Other books edited by John Bierhorst

Black Rainbow

Decorations by Jane Byers Bierhorst

FARRAR, STRAUS AND GIROUX
NEW YORK

BLACK RAINBOW

Legends of the Incas and
Myths of Ancient Peru

Edited and translated by
John Bierhorst

Library of Congress Cataloging in Publication Data

Black Rainbow | Bibliography: p. 123 | 1. Incas—Legends
2. Quechua Indians—Legends | 3. Indians of South America—Peru—Legends
I. Bierhorst, John | F3429.3.F6B55 | 398.2 | 76-19092

Acknowledgment is made for permission to translate from the following
books: *Leyendas Quechuas* by Jesús Lara, © 1960 by Jesús Lara | *El Arte
Folklórico de Bolivia* by M. Rigoberto Paredes, copyright 1949 by Antonio
Paredes-Candia | *Francisco de Avila* by Hermann Trimborn and Antje Kelm,
© 1967 Gebr. Mann Verlag, Berlin. For titles of the selections translated,
see Notes on Sources.

FRONTISPIECE | *Gold
funerary mask from the Nazca
culture of south coastal Peru*

Contents

What rainbow is this black rainbow dawning,
Dark, an arrow in the hands of Cuzco's foe?
Evil, a shower of hail!

Dreaming, waking, half waking,
My heart has glimpsed the blue fly Death,
All along and many times before.

The sun comes yellow, turns dark . . .

Apu Inca Atahuallpaman

Black Rainbow

THE INCA LAND AND INCA CULTURE

Peru, generally speaking, is uninhabitable. Its spectacular but harsh terrain, stretching from north to south in three dissimilar ribbons—a strip of coastal desert, a chain of snow-capped peaks, a somewhat broader belt of hilly jungle—remains in large part a wilderness, much as it was in Inca times.

But here and there a river finds its way across the desert, and along its banks today, as in the past, are towns and villages. At intervals throughout the highlands, which include some of the greatest peaks in the Andes, are fertile valleys supporting, in some cases, sizable populations. The Valley of Cuzco, site of the ancient Inca capital, and the nearby Yucay Valley, where Inca emperors had their country estates, are two of the best known of these favored locations.

Among the peaks south of Cuzco, high windswept plains, or *punas,* extend toward the border of present-day Bolivia and the superb alpine lake called Titicaca. No other body of water in the world is so large and so high; and as we shall see, it figures prominently in Peruvian myth and legend.

On the west the highlands drop down to the narrow strip of desert bordering the sea, while on the east they fall away in diminishing tiers of jungle-clad hills, gradually merging with the Brazilian forests beyond. Into this eastern region the Inca armies only rarely ventured, probably never penetrating more than a hundred miles, though they regularly patrolled the highlands and the coastal desert.

Because of the different meanings attached to it, the word "Inca" has been a source of confusion. Originally it must have referred only to the members of a small, inconspicuous tribe, one among many, that flourished in the southern highlands perhaps no earlier than A.D. 1200. As this group began to expand its territory, it incorporated the rulers of conquered tribes into its own system of government by making them adopted Incas, or Incas by privilege, so that in time the word "Inca" came to signify an imperial ruling class, with the emperor himself known as *the* Inca.

Many of the conquered peoples, of course, did not speak the Inca language. But in order to consolidate the empire, the Incas forced them to learn this language, which is usually called Quechua (pronounced KETCH-wa), and as a result the various native tongues fell largely into disuse. Quechua eventually became, and still is, the almost universal Indian language of highland and coastal Peru, as well as of parts of modern Ecuador, Bolivia, and Argentina. But the five million persons who speak it today cannot properly be called Incas. Inasmuch as the Inca ruling class has long since disappeared, the surviving populations are referred to as simply "the Quechua," or, with even less precision, "the Indian people of Peru."

During the days of Inca ascendancy, however, the old tribal divisions were still very much in evidence, and in the legends that have been preserved we find frequent references to such peoples as the Alcahuiza, the Lare, the Collahuaya, the Allancu, the Cana, and the Chaqui. Not to mention dozens of others, many of them quite obscure. The problems involved in holding together so many different tribes were undoubtedly great. But the Incas were more than equal to the task. Not only did they oblige conquered tribesmen to adopt the Quechua language, but in some cases they uprooted whole communities, resettling them at great distances from the home valleys they had learned to defend. Discontent was kept to a minimum by the ample supplies that flowed from imperial warehouses. No one was allowed to go hungry or unclothed.

It would appear that hostile tribes were occasionally won over by sheer promises. This kind of conquest is recalled in the fanciful legend of the rod of gold (see page 27). The legend is wholly fictitious, but the method of peaceful conquest was almost certainly an instrument of policy during the great days of the empire.

Naturally, the usual method was more violent. An imperial army with troops numbering well into the thousands would close in swiftly upon the beleaguered settlement, whose people, forewarned by scouts or messengers, would have already fled to their nearby fortress. If their own troops were sufficiently numerous, these might sally forth to meet the invaders, with the two sides exchanging hurled stones and bolas—the bola being a loose gathering of strings with weights tied to the ends, used to entangle an enemy's legs. Then followed hand-to-hand combat with lances, axes, and war clubs. In these engagements the Incas were almost always the victors.

In war as in peace the authority of the ruling class was heightened by carefully prescribed marks of prestige. Whenever they traveled, even going to battle, Inca nobles were carried in litters, or sedan chairs, the typical litter consisting of two poles with a platform between, surmounted by a stool and sometimes a canopy. This conveyance was borne along on the shoulders of four men. Not surprisingly, the Incas wore fine garments and gold and silver ornaments that were forbidden to commoners. Moreover, they were expected to pierce their earlobes, stretching the opening to accommodate the enormous disclike ear plugs that were the unmistakable mark of an Inca. When the Spaniards arrived, they called the Incas *orejones,* meaning "big ears."

Inca prestige was further enhanced by official legends like the story of the rod of gold, in which it is suggested that the Incas themselves were the originators of all the vital arts of civilization, including farming, herding, building, and weaving. Nothing, of course, could be further from the truth.

Peruvian culture is hundreds, even thousands, of years older than the Incas. Archaeologists have determined that corn, imported from Mexico, was being grown in Peru as early as 1400 B.C. And during the pre-Inca period numerous other crops had been discovered or developed, including the so-called Irish potato, which is of Peruvian origin, and a cereal known as quinoa, closely related to the pigweed.

From quinoa a kind of flour can be prepared, or the whole seeds may be used in a soup. Such a soup plays an interesting role in the myth called "The Boy Who Rose to the Sky" (page 94). Corn too, as is well known, yields a flour, or meal, from which cakes are made. But it also has other uses—for example, in the preparation of chicha, an alcoholic beverage popular in South and Central America, mentioned in the myth of the macaw woman (page 78).

Today, as formerly, the Quechua farmer breaks up the soil with a wooden-handled spade, or foot plow, called *taclla.* He sows his seeds, but does not wait for rain. Rain in coastal, and even in parts of highland, Peru is either scarce or altogether absent. Instead, he makes certain that his irrigation ditches are in order, and inevitably, today as in the remote past, there will be disputes with his neighbors over how much of the available river or spring water he can rightfully use. Odd as it may seem, the distribution of water is one of the favorite themes in Peruvian literature. In the present collection it plays a role in two legends: "Mayta Capac" (page 33) and "Utca Paucar" (page 61).

Herding is another of the ancient arts still practiced today. Although sheep brought from the Old World have been introduced in many parts of the country, the native llama, a species related to the camel, is still common, especially in the southern highlands. Hardly a difficult activity, herding is frequently left to young people, and it is perhaps for this reason that folk tales, with their typically teen-aged heroes and heroines, are, in Peru, very often concerned with llama herding.

The llama is principally a beast of burden. Its flesh is seldom eaten and the wool can be used in weaving only the coarsest fabrics. Better textiles were woven of cotton, or of wool from the alpaca or the highly prized vicuña. In ancient days the very finest cloth was known as *compi*. It was woven on special looms, using threads of different colors, sometimes with feathers worked into the fabric.

Compi is mentioned in the famous story called "The Llama Herder and the Daughter of the Sun" (page 49). The llama, predictably, is referred to in several of the stories—where one will also find references to such animals as the vicuña, the puma, the guanaco, the skunk, the condor, and the macaw. Plants are also mentioned, including not only corn, cotton, and quinoa, but the unusual rose tree, called quenual, and the cantuta, which today is the national flower of Peru. In short, both the natural environment and the cultural life of the people are abundantly evident in the myths, tales, and legends that follow.

RELIGION IN ANCIENT PERU

Like most ancient peoples, the Incas and their contemporaries worshipped multiple gods. Yet there was an unmistakable tendency for each group to recognize a single god as supremely significant, at least so far as its own tribal fortunes were concerned.

For the Incas at Cuzco this god was Inti, the sun. For the tribes of the northern coast it was Con, or Kon, also called Coniraya, the meaning of whose name is not now known. Another god of surpassing importance was Viracocha (pronounced weer-a-CO-cha), whose cult may have originated on the shores of Lake Titicaca.

As the Incas grew in prominence, they revised their traditional form of worship and made it into a state religion worthy of their imperial ambitions. Inti, the sun, remained their special protector; the sun was still believed to be the ancestor of the Inca race, with the Inca himself revered as a kind of human embodiment of the sun's power. But the god Viracocha was now called upon to function as ultimate Creator. According to the new teaching, Viracocha had created all things, including the sun. Lofty prayers were composed in his honor, and he was given such names as Ticsi, meaning "foundation," and Pachayachachic, "instructor of the world."

The original meaning of the name Viracocha was perhaps already lost by Inca times. But there are indications that at least some native thinkers interpreted it to mean "foam of the sea," from *vira* ("fat" or "grease") and *cocha* ("sea").

The cult of Viracocha became the official religion of the empire. But the manner in which it was adapted to the worship of ineradicable local gods varied from place to place. The divinity Coniraya, for example, was simply identified with Viracocha, who was then recognized in certain regions as Coniraya Viracocha or as Con Ticsi Viracocha.

In the province of Huarochirí in the central highlands the local god Pariacaca came to be regarded, not as identical with Viracocha, but as Viracocha's son. Pariacaca and *his* son, Macahuisa, are the principal divinities mentioned in the legend of Topa Inca and the storm (page 37). The

9

legend shows how the Inca came to respect these gods and to pay them homage.

Two other local gods, of even greater fame, were Catiquilla, worshipped at Huamachuco in the northern highlands, and the formidable Pachacamac, whose shrine was near the present-day seacoast town of Lurín, about twenty miles south of Lima. Both Catiquilla and Pachacamac were well-known oracles. That is, their statues were supposed to answer questions, give advice, and predict the future. In some cases at least, the prophecy was spoken by a priest hiding behind the idol. A legend concerning Catiquilla, the oracle at Huamachuco, is given on pages 47–8.

It is interesting to note that ancient Peruvian religion, like Catholicism, included the confession of sins. It also included a convent system, whereby certain women, who were forbidden to marry or have relations with men, lived apart in carefully guarded communal houses. These women are usually referred to as "sun maidens" or "daughters of the sun."

DESIGNING THE WORLD

The Incas imagined that their capital city of Cuzco was shaped like a mountain lion. The fortress that stood at the top of the valley was supposed to be the lion's head. The point just below the Temple of the Sun, where two small rivers join, was the lion's tail. The great square in the center of the city was its heart. And so forth.

The citizens themselves, however, were supposed to

represent a pair of siblings. Those who lived in Upper
Cuzco were regarded as the "brother." Lower Cuzco was
the "sister." It was also said that the two groups were like
two arms: one left, the other right.

Typical of the American Indian tendency to give the
physical and social world a meaningful design, such
images would appear to have been more common in
ancient Peru than elsewhere. Vast areas of the coastal
desert south of Lima are etched with man-made lines, sun-
burst and even animal designs so gigantic that they cannot
be properly viewed except from an airplane. The city of
Cuzco itself lies at the center of more than three hundred
shrines arranged over the surrounding hillsides in a system of radiating lines.

We cannot be sure what these enormous earth patterns
signified. But we do know that the Incas conceived of the
physical world in its entirety as a cruciform design with
Cuzco at its center. The arms of the cross were the four
main highways originating in Cuzco's central plaza, or
great square, each extending toward one of the four
quarters of the realm. Thus the Inca empire was known as
Tahuantinsuyu, "Land of the Four Quarters."

In the legend of the vanishing bride (page 42) we
have an example of the social world similarly systematized.
In this poignant story the Inca, anticipating the Spanish
Conquest, calls his subjects together and has them bring
up out of the depths of the earth the mystic bride who
represents the life of the people; taking her as his wife,
he disappears, never to return. But in order to fully appre-
ciate the significance of the tragedy we must notice that

the Inca's subjects, whom he leaves behind, are divided into three groups: condor people, hawk people, and swallow people. The condor, as is widely believed, is a bird of the highest mountaintops, always associated with the sky in Peruvian lore. The hawk is a bird of lower elevations, while swallows, or at least some of them, preferring riverbanks and cliffsides, actually make their nests within the earth. (This is why the swallow must play the leading role in fetching up the mystic bride.) We may therefore conjecture that the three birds represent the sky, the earth's surface, and the underworld—that is, the three levels of the universe, or the universe in its entirety.

It is certainly not true that Peruvian society under the Incas was divided into three bird-ancestor groups. Though the scheme may in fact have been suggested by the clan system of a particular local tribe, as presented here it must be viewed as an imaginary design used to give the legend its sense of universal doom. In other words, the disaster is magnified so that it appears as though the world itself is coming to an end. And for Inca society this is very much the way things must have seemed.

INCA HISTORY

Although the Incas had no written records, it would be an oversimplification to say that their history was handed down by word of mouth. At Cuzco there is reported to have been a series of painted panels which must have served as a reference for scholars whose duty it was to remember the past. Possibly these painted "books" were supplemented by the mysterious *quipus,* or knotted strings, which were undoubtedly used to preserve arithmetical data such as warehouse inventories and census figures but which might also have contained war records and genealogies.

The historical accounts themselves, partly factual, partly legendary, were composed in verse, which made them easier to remember. Unfortunately, none has survived in the original form. But Spanish chroniclers who heard them during the first few decades after the Conquest and who wove them into European-style histories have left us a reasonably trustworthy record of the rise and fall of the empire and its succession of rulers. These rulers, or Incas, are here listed in order:

1 | Manco Capac (probably legendary)
2 | Sinchi Roca (ruled about A.D. 1250)
3 | Lloque Yupanqui
4 | Mayta Capac
5 | Capac Yupanqui
6 | Inca Roca
7 | Yahuar Huacac
8 | Viracocha Inca
9 | Pachacuti (ruled 1438–71)
10 | Topa Inca Yupanqui
11 | Huayna Capac (died 1525)
12 | Huascar (died 1532)
13 | Atahualpa (died 1533)

Under its first six or seven rulers the Inca state remained insignificantly small. Not until the reign of Viracocha Inca did it begin to expand beyond the Valley of Cuzco. It was the ninth ruler, Pachacuti, however, who became the true father of the empire. Under Pachacuti and his son, Topa Inca Yupanqui, the realm was extended to Quito in the north, site of the capital of present-day Ecuador, and the Maule River in the south, halfway down the coast of modern Chile—a span of 2,500 miles.

Rumors of white, bearded strangers began to reach Cuzco in the time of the eleventh Inca, Huayna Capac. Had Pizarro and his tiny band of fewer than two hundred men attempted to conquer Peru during the reign of this Inca, they might not have succeeded so easily. But when the campaign was at last begun, in 1532, Huayna Capac had died, leaving the realm divided between his warring sons, Huascar and Atahualpa.

At first the empire fell to Huascar, but was wrested from him by the armies of Atahualpa. Then, in an astonishingly brief struggle at Cajamarca in the central highlands, the newly arrived Spaniards succeeded in capturing Atahualpa himself, keeping him alive for nearly a year while they extorted gold from his subjects. Though the ransom was paid in full, the prisoner was not released. Atahualpa was finally murdered by Pizarro's men on August 29, 1533, and with no Inca at the helm, Huascar having been executed the year before by Atahualpa's adherents, the empire swiftly went under.

Modern historians agree that the sudden downfall of the Incas had much to do with the civil war between Huascar and Atahualpa. No doubt it did. The myths and legends, however, tell a somewhat different story.

To begin with, we must take note of two rather curious facts about the Incas. One is the custom by which the emperor took his own sister as his queen, or Coya. The other is the manner in which the Incas accepted, even institutionalized, the evil of unbridled aggression.

The brother-sister marriage is mentioned casually in the legend of the rod of gold (page 27), as though nothing could have been more natural to a highborn Inca. The truth is that the emperors were using their royal privilege to undermine what is probably one of the strictest of all taboos. Though the unmentionable sin is never spelled out, it is no doubt the real subject of the innocent-appearing legend of the llama herder and the daughter of the sun (page 49). The llama herder is really the Inca, and the daughter of the sun is his sister. We can tell this by examining a number of interesting clues in the story itself, some of which the reader will be able to discover. I will simply call attention to one rather obscure detail: the hero's name, given as Acoynapa, from *acoy,* meaning "evil" or "accursed," and *napa,* meaning "white llama," which was a symbol of the emperor. Thus the llama herder is the "accursed Inca," and the legend as a whole may be read as an allegory of the downfall of the empire, brought about by the guilty behavior of its ruler.

The question of unbridled aggression is raised in the legend of Mayta Capac (page 33), the warlike Inca who embodied cruelty. Certainly no empire can thrive or expand without ruthlessness, but the accusatory tone of this legend makes it clear that the Incas had a measure of guilt about such behavior.

Like Mayta Capac, all the subsequent Inca emperors were cruel. Atahualpa, however, had the misfortune of leading the empire to its ruin; and to him, therefore, are ascribed cruelties supposedly unprecedented. The legend of the oracle at Huamachuco (page 47), a typical example, suggests that Atahualpa's defeat came about as divine punishment for his outrageous looting and murdering.

But not all native Peruvians have turned their anger inward. Many did and still do regard Atahualpa as a martyr, and the tide of hatred for the descendants of the Spanish conquerors has by no means been stemmed even today. Such sentiments are expressed in the anonymous Quechua poem *Apu Inca Atahuallpaman,* the opening lines of which have been taken as the epigraph to this book.

LITERATURE

The oral literature of native Peru, strictly speaking, has not been well preserved. The Spanish chroniclers of the sixteenth century have left us relatively little. Regrettably, with the exception of certain prayers recorded by Cristóbal de Molina of Cuzco and by Juan de Santacruz Pachacuti, none of the old court literature can now be studied in the Quechua language.

Perhaps the best source for reconstructing the bardic legends would be the chronicler Sarmiento de Gamboa, whose Spanish text appears in a few passages to be an almost literal translation from the Quechua. An outstanding example is the tale of Mayta Capac (page 33), where we may still feel the rhythmic pulse of the original chant and take note of characteristic rhetorical devices. One of these is the double name given to the Alcahuiza tribe, written "the Alcahuiza and Culunchima tribes" in Sarmiento's version. A much better translation might have been simply "the Alcahuizas, the Culunchimas," because it is obvious from the story that "Culunchima" is merely another name for the Alcahuizas. This kind of double naming is typical of American Indian bardic literature.

Additional legends of good quality are preserved in the writings of Martín de Morúa, Juan de Betanzos, Garcilaso de la Vega, and others. But these have been so completely recast in the Spanish idiom that they no longer carry the flavor of Quechua narrative. They must be read for subject matter only, not for style.

Easily the finest material that has survived is the late-sixteenth-century manuscript of Francisco de Avila, containing myths and legends actually recorded in the Quechua language. Although this material was collected in the province of Huarochirí and therefore cannot be regarded as typical of the court literature of Cuzco, it nevertheless displays much intellectual refinement and a characteristically vigorous mythic style.

Modern collections of Quechua folklore have on the whole been disappointing. The custom of rewriting in flowery phrases, begun by the old chroniclers, has by no means disappeared. Often it is hard to tell where the native thought leaves off and the compiler's embellishment begins. Even so, the material is not without interest, and a few genuinely fine tales have been recorded.

In approaching these varied sources, I have adopted a varying standard of English translation: in general, the better the source, the more literal the translation. My translations from Avila's manuscript (pages 37, 42, and 72) are as scrupulously literal as I can make them. I have treated Sarmiento with utmost respect, merely eliminating a few passages that were clearly extraneous. Morúa likewise (page 49), despite the fact that he uses a rather heavy Spanish idiom. In other cases I have sometimes trimmed excess verbiage, sometimes not. The degree of freedom can be judged by the terms used in the notes at the back of the book, listed here in order of descending literalness: "translated," "translated, with omissions," "freely translated," "adapted."

For the purposes of this anthology I make the following distinctions: a "legend" is the fantastic interpretation of a historical event; a "myth" is a story, not necessarily sacred, which incorporates important articles of belief; relatively simpler stories told for entertainment or to point a moral are classed as "tales" or "fables." Needless to say, these categories are not clear-cut.

Of the twenty stories included, half were recorded during the period 1533–1608, when Inca traditions were presumably fresh in the minds of native informants. All the stories given in the sections entitled "Legends of the Incas" and "Myths of Ancient Peru" belong to this category. The four stories grouped under the heading "Myths That Have Survived" may also lay claim to ancient status, despite the fact that they were collected in the twentieth century. These stories come from remote villages and are remarkably similar to other, non-Andean, Indian myths that are known to be very old.

The story I have labeled "A Latter-Day Legend," though it claims to be Inca, or even pre-Inca, would appear to be a European-style treatment of a basic theme that may nonetheless be old; it was written down in the twentieth century. As for the section entitled "Modern Fables and Animal Tales," these stories pose something of a problem. Though they have a strong Andean flavor, folklorists are not convinced that they derive from other than European models.

Thus the collection as a whole is a representative sampling of the Andean storyteller's art, with preference given to material that is either definitely Inca or as close to it as we can now get.

THE MYTH OF CONIRAYA
AND CAHUILLACA

With the exception of the very poorly preserved Viracocha epic (page 69), the story of Coniraya and Cahuillaca is probably the best known of all Peruvian myths. Certainly it is one of the most elegant—and most difficult.

On the assumption that a close examination of this myth will be repaid by a deeper understanding of Peruvian myth in general, I would like to suggest that the reader take a look at the story itself (page 72) and then bear with me for a few more paragraphs.

Perhaps the first thing to be mentioned is that the myth belongs to a widespread American Indian literary form which I shall call *double myth*. A double myth is a myth that repeats itself; in other words, it tells the same story twice. And it is for this reason that I have taken the liberty of dividing the text into two parts, labeled I and II.

In each of the two parts the same plot, or argument, is set forth. Part I tells it from a woman's point of view; Part II tells it from a man's. The argument, as I see it, runs as follows:

A man's or a woman's duty in life is to marry and reproduce. To do so, one must cross over from childhood to adulthood. One must become a provider and cause the natural world to produce food—and shelter and clothing and all the other cultural necessities. This in turn requires that the world of nature be set in order, made comprehensible. Gardens must be laid out, towns established, society organized, and distinctions made between good and evil. The responsibilities, needless to say, are great. Perhaps it would be easier to remain a child. Perhaps it would be better not to have fallen in love in the first place. Love perhaps is fraught with danger. Perhaps it is unclean, impure. In short, though it would be thoroughly irresponsible, it would indeed be easier to remain a child.

What we have, then, is a love story, if an unhappy one. But the love story is also a myth about growing up. The heroine, whatever her age, reminds us of a maiden at puberty. No man has succeeded in touching her, we are told, yet she is ripe for marriage. As for the hero, Coniraya, he is no doubt ageless. Yet in his flight from the high-lands to the lowlands in pursuit of the heroine he behaves like a boy about to become a man. It was, in fact, a part of the puberty ritual in ancient Peru for boys to race down from a mountaintop in pursuit of young women (who would await them with jars of the alcoholic beverage called chicha).

But in our story the fleeing heroine escapes entirely and becomes immobilized in a world inhabited by her own sex. The hero, likewise, at the close of Part II, flees the low-land world of women and returns to the highlands, where, as we have seen, the actors are men. So the sexes remain separate. Moreover, they remain childlike. Cahuillaca, in effect, has returned to her mother, who now goes "look-ing" for her. Coniraya, whose final role is to make "fun" of people, has become a trickster, the mythic counter-part of the irresponsible child.

Both the hero and the heroine have experimented with, and evidently rejected, adult responsibilities. Cahuillaca has borne a child, and in her ability to weave she has demonstrated that she can be a provider. Coniraya, for his part, has fathered a child. He too is a provider, having filled the sea with fish. Moreover, he has set the world in order, creating at the beginning of Part I a system of aqueducts and terraced hillsides and at the beginning of Part II a universal framework of good and evil.

But something is wrong. The heroine is unable to accept the hero for what he is. She finds him unclean. We see this in Part I and again in Part II, where the heroine reappears not as Cahuillaca but as the two daughters of

21

the fearsome mother. The elder daughter, who sleeps with Coniraya, represents the heroine's repugnance upon discovering the identity of the child's father; the younger daughter, who becomes a dove, represents the purity she would like to maintain. As in Old World lore, the dove in Peruvian myth is a symbol of innocence. Coniraya, in his turn, discovers, or at least imagines, that women can be murderous.

In Coniraya's case the fear is fear of death. Everyone has heard that love and death are in some way connected, and in the ancient myths the connection is often made quite clear. Here it is only hinted. But the inescapable truth is that falling in love and becoming a parent necessarily mean that the parent will be replaced; only by remaining a child can love—and death—be avoided.

The story, perhaps, does not seem sad, because like all good myths it is not sentimentalized. But let us look at more or less the same plot in a different dress. There are, in fact, five other examples of it in the present collection.

In "The Condor Seeks a Wife" and in "The Boy Who Rose to the Sky" the tragedy is made obvious for us by what would appear to be an added dose of European sentimentality. In the excellent folk tale called "The Mouse Husband" it is made both humorous and macabre. In "The Dancing Fox" it is simply humorous.

Of course the mythic love story does not have to be a tragedy. In "The Macaw Woman" (page 78) it is presented as a triumph. But sifting through the myths and tales that have been preserved, one is struck by what seems to be a generally negative view of life's possibilities. Various writers have commented on this point, some even suggesting that the supposed melancholy of Peruvian folklore has to do with the Conquest and its legacy of unresolved despair. Without completely rejecting this theory, I would prefer to point out that the world view incorporated in Inca and latter-day Peruvian literature is not merely plaintive but uncompromisingly realistic. It is by turns salty, grim, austere, or poignant, and as such contributes a thoroughly harmonious, if striking, coloration to the mainstream of American Indian lore.

Llama motif from a woven bag of the Nazca culture, south coastal Peru

LEGENDS OF THE INCAS

The Rod of Gold

In ages long past there was nothing but wilderness and the people lived like beasts. There were no villages, no houses, and no cultivated fields. No one wore proper clothes, for as yet they did not know how to weave cotton or wool. They lived in twos or threes wherever they chanced to find shelter, beneath overhanging rocks or in caves in the ground. Like animals they ate wild plants and the roots of trees, also fruits that grew without cultivation; and they ate human flesh. They covered their bodies with leaves and bark and furs, and some even went unclothed. They were like deer, like creatures of the wild, and like beasts they had no regular marriages, but lived with first one and then another.

But Our Father the Sun took pity on them and sent down from the sky his own son and daughter to teach them the worship of the Sun, to give them laws to live by, and to show them how to build villages, grow crops, and tend livestock.

Our Father the Sun sent his two children down to Lake Titicaca and ordered them to proceed from there in any direction they chose. But wherever they stopped to eat or sleep they were to push in the ground a rod of gold, half the length of a man's arm and two fingers thick, which he had given them as a sacred sign. Wherever the rod could be made to disappear in the earth with a single thrust, then there in that place they would found their city and their royal court. His parting words were these:

"When all the people have been made your subjects, you must rule them wisely and justly, with pity, with mercy, and with tenderness. I want you to treat them as a compassionate father would his beloved children, and in this you must imitate and resemble me, for it is I who take care of the world and give it light and warmth, making pastures and fields grow green, making trees give fruit, and livestock bear offspring; making rain and fair weather, and not failing to pass through the sky each day to see what the people might need and to aid them and comfort them, being their provider and their benefactor. As you are my son and my daughter, you must be like me. You

28

must go into the world and provide for these people who have lived like beasts. I therefore establish and name you rulers over all those races whom you will lift up with your good instruction, good works, and lawful government."

When Our Father the Sun had spoken his will, he took leave of his two children; then they came forth from the waters of Lake Titicaca and traveled northward. Wherever they stopped along the way, they tried to drive the rod of gold into the earth. But they could not make it disappear. At last they entered a little shelter, or resting place, called House of the Dawn. It was given this name because our lord, the Inca, emerged from it just at dawn, and from there he proceeded with his wife and sister, our Coya, to the Valley of Cuzco, which at that time was a wild and rugged land.

The first stop they made in this valley was at the hill called Rainbow, on the south side of the present city. There they tried the earth with the rod of gold, and with a single stroke they drove it in and it was not seen again. Then our Inca said to his wife and sister:

"Our Father the Sun commands us to stop in this valley and build our city so that we may carry out his wishes. Let us each go in a different direction and gather the people together. We will give them instructions and begin the work Our Father the Sun has ordered us to do."

Then our first rulers went out from the hill called Rainbow, and the Inca went north and the Coya went south. As they proceeded through the wilderness they told all the men and women they met how their Father the Sun had sent them from the sky to be rulers and benefactors, to bring the people out of the wilds and thickets, to teach them to live in towns, and to give them proper food.

The people were astonished to see the fine clothes and adornments Our Father the Sun had given his two children. And they saw the pierced earlobes, greatly stretched, that we Incas who are their descendants still have today, and they saw in their faces and could tell by their manner of speaking that they were indeed the Sun's children, come to provide towns that the people might live in and food that they might eat; and these promises made them eager. They believed what they were told and adored the Inca and the Coya and worshipped them as children of the Sun and obeyed them as rulers.

The people discussed it among themselves. They spoke of the marvelous things they were seeing and hearing. Then they assembled in a great throng and followed where our rulers led them.

When our royal leaders saw how many people had gathered around them, they ordered some to provide food from the field so that they would not again be dispersed by hunger. They ordered others to build houses by copying a model that the Inca himself gave them. In this way our imperial city of Cuzco came to be populated, and it was divided into halves, called Upper Cuzco and Lower Cuzco. Those who had been summoned by the Inca were settled in the upper half, while the lower half was reserved for those who had been brought by the Coya. The two halves lived together as equals, as brother and sister, as left arm and right arm. And all the towns and villages that were founded later were divided likewise.

When the city had been established, our Inca showed all the men what their particular duties would be. He showed them how to break the earth and till it, how to sow corn and quinoa and all the many vegetables; and he showed them which ones were good to eat and nourishing. He showed them how to make the foot plow and the other tools they would need, and how to divert streams and make canals to irrigate their fields. He even taught them to make sandals.

Meanwhile, the Coya instructed the women, taught them to spin cotton and wool, to weave, and to make clothes for themselves and for their husbands and sons. She showed them how to perform all the duties of the home. And so our rulers taught their first subjects everything pertaining to human life, and the Inca was master of men and the Coya was mistress of women.

Then the people saw that they were changed and that they had received great benefits. Joyfully they went out into the mountains to spread the news about the Sun's children and to tell all those they met about the wonderful things that had happened. As proof they brought with them their new clothes and their new food, and they told how they were living in houses. The people of the wilds gathered in great numbers and came to see for themselves what our first parents had done. When they were satisfied that what they had been told was true, they stayed on and served the Inca and the Coya and obeyed them.

In this way the word was passed from mouth to mouth, and in a few years an enormous number of people had been brought together, enough so that in six or seven years' time the Inca was able to form an army to defend himself and also to bring in by force those who would not come willingly. He taught the use of bows and arrows, spears, clubs, and other weapons that are still known today.

To tell you briefly of the deeds of our first Inca, I will only mention that toward the east he established his control as far as the river called House of Many Colors, and on the west his lands extended 32,000 paces toward the river called Great Speaker. In the south he won 36,000 paces toward Quequesana, and in that region our Inca built a hundred towns, the largest of which had a hundred houses, the others being smaller according to the natural advantages of each site.

These, then, were the first beginnings of the city you see today. These were the beginnings of our great empire. And these were our first rulers, from whom our later rulers were descended. Our first Inca was called Manco Capac, and our Coya was Mama Ocllo. They were brother and sister, as I have told you. And they were children of the Sun and the Moon.

Mayta Capac

The Inca Lloque Yupanqui had grown old without an heir.
And now it was widely believed that he was too old, too
weak, to father a child.

Yet one day as he sat grieving, deep in sorrow, the Sun
appeared to him in human form and consoled him, saying,
"Do not grieve, Lloque Yupanqui, for your descendants
shall be great lords. You shall father a child."

Upon hearing this, the Inca reported it to his kinsmen,
who in turn made it known to the people. Then they set

about to find him a wife. It was his own brother, being the one who knew best the Inca's nature, who selected the bride. He found her in the town of Oma, asked permission of her relatives, obtained her, and brought her to Cuzco. This woman was called Mama Caua, and by her the Inca was to have a son, whose name would be Mayta Capac.

Mama Caua had been pregnant only three months when her son was born. He was born with teeth. He was lively. And so quickly did he grow that at the end of one year he was as large and as strong as an eight-year-old. By the time he was two he was fighting with young men and could beat them and injure them severely.

They say that he joined in games with certain youths of the Alcahuiza, the Culunchima tribe, who lived in the vicinity of Cuzco; and he hurt a great many of them, and some were even killed. One day, in a dispute over who might drink water from a particular fountain, he broke the leg of the son of the Alcahuizas' chief lord, and he chased the other boys into their houses, where indeed the Alcahuizas had been living in peace without troubling the Incas.

At last the Alcahuizas could no longer endure the attacks of Mayta Capac. And though they knew he was the Inca's favorite and well guarded by his kinsmen, they were nonetheless prepared to kill him. They were ready to risk their lives. They selected ten among themselves, and these were sent to the House of the Sun, where Lloque Yupanqui and Mayta Capac lived.

As they entered, intending to kill them both, it happened that Mayta Capac was playing ball with some other boys in the palace court. When he saw his enemies arriving, bearing arms, he hurled a ball in their direction, and one of them was hit and killed. Then he attacked the others and made them flee; and although they escaped, they fled with many wounds. This then is how they returned to their chief lord.

When the Alcahuizas, the Culunchimas, were made aware of the injury that had been done to their people, they were filled with fear. Mayta Capac was only a child. What might he do when he became a man?

Now, truly, they were prepared to risk their lives. Gathering all their people together, they set out to make war against the Incas.

Then Lloque Yupanqui was troubled. He feared he would be destroyed, and he reprimanded his son, Mayta Capac, saying, "Child! Why have you injured these people? I am an old man. Would you have me die at the hands of our enemies?"

But the Inca's own subjects, who loved to pillage, who preferred war over peace and lived by thievery, spoke up in favor of Mayta Capac and told the Inca to keep still and not to speak against his son. Then indeed Lloque Yupanqui no longer reprimanded his son.

The Alcahuizas, the Culunchimas, prepared their troops. Mayta Capac likewise took command of his subjects. Both sides gave battle, and though at first the contest was even, with neither side prevailing, then at last when each party had fought long, each hoping to win the victory, the Alcahuizas, the Culunchimas, were defeated by the subjects of Mayta Capac.

But the Alcahuizas were not disheartened. They came again and with greater spirit. They attacked the House of the Sun and pounded it on three sides. At first Mayta Capac, having retired to his quarters, was unaware of what had happened. But then he emerged. He came out from behind the walls. He struggled fiercely with his enemies, and at last he routed them, he defeated them. Then he danced, adorning himself with fine regalia.

Still the Alcahuizas would not desist. Again they called Mayta Capac to battle, and again he accepted. But they say that now a hailstorm fell on the Alcahuizas, so that all of them were finally defeated. Then Mayta Capac took their chief lord and kept him in prison until he died.

Indeed this Mayta Capac was bold. He was the first since the days of Manco Capac to take up arms and win victories.

And they say that Mayta Capac inherited the Sun bird that Manco Capac had brought with him when he founded Cuzco. Always the bird had been locked within a hamper of woven reeds, handed down from Inca to Inca, and no one had ventured to open it, for all were timid.

But Mayta Capac was more daring than they. He wished to see what his forebears had kept so carefully hidden. He opened the hamper. He took out the Sun bird and spoke to it. Truly, they say, it answered him in oracles. And because of it he grew wise. He knew what would happen: he could foretell the future.

The Storm

When Topa Inca Yupanqui was lord and had conquered many provinces, then for a long time he rested in great contentment.

But finally and in different places there came a rebellion of the Allancu, the Callancu, and the Chaqui. These tribes would not be subjects of the Inca.

And so the Inca fought with them for twelve years, enlisting many thousands of his people, all of whom, however, were destroyed. Then the Inca mourned. He was deeply troubled, thinking, "What will become of us?"

Then one day he thought to himself, "Why do I offer the gods my gold and silver, my woven robes, my food, and everything else that I have? What do they do for me? Now, this moment, I will send for them so that they can help me against these rebels." Then he spoke aloud and summoned them with the words: "Wherever you are, come, you who receive gold and silver!"

Then the gods said yes and they came.

Pachacamac came in a litter, and so too, in litters, did the other gods come from every part of Tahuantinsuyu, and they all came together in the great square at Cuzco.

Pariacaca, however, had not yet arrived. "Should I go? Or should I not go?" He was unable to make up his mind. Then at last he sent his son, Macahuisa, saying, "Go! And listen!"

When Macahuisa arrived, he sat down in the rear next to his litter.

Then the Inca began to speak: "O Fathers! Gods and Spirits! You know already how I have made you sacrificial offerings of gold and silver. My heart has been filled with devotion. And seeing that I have served you well, could you not come to my aid, now that I am losing so many thousands of my people? It is for this that I have called you."

But when he had spoken, not a one gave him answer. They merely sat there saying nothing. Then the Inca spoke again: "Speak! You made and created these people. Will you let them die in battle? Help me! Or I will have you all burned on the spot. Why should I serve and adorn you with gold and silver, with food by the basketful and drink, with llamas of mine, and everything else that I have? You hear my sorrow, and if you will not aid me, or even speak, you must burn on the spot." These were his words.

Then Pachacamac began to speak: "Inca, O Rising Sun, I who can violently shake all things, even you and the whole earth—I have not yet spoken, for were I to destroy these rebels, then you too and even the earth would likewise be destroyed. And so I sit here saying nothing."

Then at last, though the remaining spirits kept their silence, the one who was called Macahuisa began to speak: "Inca, O Rising Sun, I will go forth! You will remain behind and watch over your subjects and protect them with your thoughts. I will go at once. For your sake I will conquer!"

As he spoke, metal poured from his mouth like an out-flowing vapor; and there before him were golden panpipes. He blew on the panpipes and made music. Also he had a flute, and it too was of gold. Upon his head he wore a headdress. His staff was gold. His tunic was black.

Then, so that Macahuisa could go, the Inca gave him one of his own litters and selected strong litter bearers from among the Collahuaya, who in but few days could cover many days' distance.

And so they carried Macahuisa in a litter against the enemy.

When they had brought him to a little mountain, Macahuisa, being Pariacaca's son, began to make it rain, at first gently. And the people living in the villages below thought, "What is this?" and prepared themselves for the worst.

Then Macahuisa flashed lightning and made more and more rain until all the villages were carried away in a flood; and where the villages had been, he made gullies. With lightning he destroyed their overlord and all their nobles. Only a few of the people were saved, but had he willed it, he could have destroyed them all. Having conquered them totally, he led the remaining survivors back to Cuzco.

From that time on, the Inca revered Pariacaca even more than he had before and furnished him with fifty attendants to make him sacrificial offerings.

Then to Pariacaca's son he spoke: "Father Macahuisa, what can I give you? Whatever you wish, demand it of me! Anything!" These were his words.

But the god answered, "I will have nothing at all, only that you worship me as our sons from Jauja do."

Then the Inca said, "Very well, Father." But he was filled with fear, thinking, "Perhaps he could destroy me too," and therefore he wished to make him an offering of anything whatsoever. And so he said, "Eat, Father!" and gave him food.

But Macahuisa replied, saying, "I am not accustomed to eating food. Bring me coral!" Then he gave him coral, and he ate it at once with a crunching sound: *cop-cop.*

Though he asked for nothing else, the Inca presented him with sun maidens. But he did not take them.

And so Macahuisa set off for home to report to his father, Pariacaca. And after that, the Incas in later days would come to worship in Jauja and dance dances of veneration.

The Vanishing Bride

Shortly before the arrival of the whites, Coniraya Viracocha betook himself to Cuzco, where he met with the Inca
Huayna Capac; and he said to him:

"My son, let us be off to Titicaca. There I will reveal
to you who and what I am."

When they got there, he spoke again: "Inca, summon
your people, that we may send forth to the Underworld
all the magicians and all those who are wise." He spoke,

and at once the Inca gave out the command.

Then his people arrived, some saying, "I am created of the condor," others saying, "I am created of the hawk," still others, "I fly like the swallow."

Then Coniraya gave them this order: "Go to the Underworld! Say to my father, 'Your son has sent me. Let me have one of his sisters.' This, then, is what you must say," he commanded.

Then he who was created of the swallow, together with the other created beings, set out for the Underworld, to return in five days.

Now it was he, the swallow man, who got there first; and when he had arrived and had delivered his message, he was given a small chest, together with the following command:

"Do not open this. The lord Huayna Capac himself must open it first," he was ordered.

But while this man was carrying the chest and when he had nearly reached Cuzco, he thought to himself, "I will see what it really is." Then he opened it, and there before him was a lady, very delicate and pretty. Her hair was wavy, it was like gold. She wore a splendid garment, and as she lay in the chest she was very small.

But the moment he saw her, she vanished. Then he arrived in Cuzco, very troubled; and Coniraya said to him, "Were you not created of the swallow, I would have you killed at once. Turn around, go back!"

Then he went back to the Underworld and brought her forth again. Along the way, as he was bringing her, whenever he felt hungry and thirsty, he would merely speak the word and at once a table would be spread out before him and a place to sleep.

And so he delivered her in just five days. And when he arrived with her, Coniraya and the Inca received her with great joy.

But before the chest was opened, Coniraya spoke out, crying, "Inca! We will leave this world," and he pointed, saying, "I will go to this land," and he pointed again, saying, "You and my sister will go to that land. You and I will never see one another again."

Then they opened the chest. The moment they opened it the earth was aglow.

Then the Inca Huayna Capac uttered these words: "Never will I return from this place. Only here will I live with my sun maiden, my queen." Then to one of his vassals and kinsmen he gave this command: "You! Go in my place! And say, 'I am Huayna Capac'! Now return to Cuzco!"

And in that moment he and his bride disappeared, and so too did Coniraya.

Then some time later, when the supposed Huayna Capac was dead, his successors began quarreling among themselves. They fought over who would be ruler, each saying, "I am first," and it was then that the whites arrived in Cajamarca.

A Messenger in Black

After a hard-fought campaign in the northern provinces, where certain rebel armies had at last been driven back, the Inca Huayna Capac withdrew to the town of Quito in order to rest and to issue new laws and new commands. At this time he received word of a pestilence raging in Cuzco. But again he pushed on, moving northward now against the tribesmen of Pasto and even beyond. As he continued his march, there were sudden bolts of lightning, striking close beside him, and convinced that these were an evil omen he turned back toward Quito.

Again he set out, marching westward toward the sea. But there, at the hour of midnight, he had a vision, in which he saw himself surrounded by millions upon millions of men. No one knows who they were. The Inca believed they were souls of the living, sent to warn him that a great many people would die of the pestilence. But the souls announced that they had come against the Inca himself and by this he understood that they were enemies and he saw that they were armed and hostile. He marched no more, but returned to Quito, and it was there that he celebrated the December feast called Capac Raymi.

Just at the dinner hour there came to him a messenger dressed in a black cloak. With great reverence he kissed the Inca and placed in his hands a small chest, its lid sealed. The Inca ordered him to open it, but the messenger excused himself, saying that it was the command of the Creator that the Inca himself must be the one to remove the cover. The Inca believed him, and as he opened the chest, out came a scattering swarm of moths and butterflies, and this was the pestilence. Within two days the chief of all the Inca's armies and many of his captains were dead, their faces covered with scabs.

When the Inca saw what had happened, he ordered a sepulcher carved out of stone, and when it was finished he placed himself in it, and there he died. When eight days had passed, the Inca's body, partly rotted, was taken out and mummified and carried home to Cuzco in a litter as though it were alive. This Inca left behind him in Quito a son named Atahualpa.

The Oracle at Huamachuco

The Inca Atahualpa was inordinately cruel. He murdered left and right. He razed. He burned. Whatever stood in his way he destroyed. As he marched from Quito to Huamachuco he committed the worst cruelties, ravages, and tyrannical abuses that had ever been known in this land.

When he reached Huamachuco he sent two of his chief lords to make sacrifices to the idol that presided there and to question it as to his future success. The lords went and made their sacrifices, but when they consulted the oracle they were told that Atahualpa would come to an evil end as punishment for his cruelty and bloodshed.

Then the lords went and told the Inca what the idol had said and the Inca was enraged. Summoning his warriors, he started toward the temple where the idol was kept. As he drew near, he armed himself with a golden ax and advanced with the two lords who had made the sacrifice.

When he reached the entrance to the temple, out came an aged priest, more than a hundred years old, dressed in a long, shaggy robe tangled with seashells, which reached to his feet. This was the priest of the oracle, and it was he who had spoken the prophecy. So informed, Atahualpa raised the ax and with a single blow cut off the old man's head.

Then he entered the little temple, and the idol too he struck with the ax; he chopped off its head, although it was made of stone. Then he ordered the old priest's body set on fire and also the idol and its temple. When all had been burned, there was nothing but ashes, and these he allowed to fly off with the wind.

The Llama Herder and the
Daughter of the Sun

Along the slopes of the snow-capped peak called Sahuasi-ray, high above the valley of the Yucay River, there lived a native Indian of the Lare tribe, called Acoynapa, a handsome and most charming young man who tended the white llamas used by the Incas as sacrificial offerings to the Sun. As he followed his grazing herd, he would play softly and sweetly upon a flute that he carried, untroubled by the amorous adventures youth is inclined to and free even from the desire for love.

49

One day, as he was playing his flute, he was approached by two daughters of the Sun, come out from one of the dwelling places that are found throughout the land and where these young women are sheltered and carefully guarded. During the day they may walk out and see the green fields and go wherever they wish, but they must always return to their houses at nightfall, and as they enter they are examined by their guards and keepers to make certain they have not brought anything with them that could do them harm. As we have said, these two came up to the llama herder as he was playing his flute, and as they stood before him they began asking him about his flock and his fields.

The startled herdsman had not even noticed their approach and fell at once to his knees, believing that these were two of the four crystal-clear fountains, famous throughout the realm, now appearing before him in human form; and he was speechless. But they continued to ask him about his llamas, telling him not to be afraid. They told him they were daughters of the Sun, mistresses of all the land, and to reassure him they took him by the arm and told him once again that there was nothing to fear.

At last the herdsman rose to his feet. Still awestruck by the great beauty of the two young women, he kissed their hands, and after conversing calmly with them at some length, he asked to be excused, saying it was time for him to gather his llamas. In order to prolong the conversation, the elder of the two maidens, whose name was Chuquillanto and who had been much taken by the manner and appearance of this young herdsman, asked him to tell her his name and where his home was. He answered that he was a member of the Lare tribe and that his name was Acoynapa. As he spoke, her eyes were drawn to his forehead, where a piece of silver, usually called campu by the Indians, gleamed and shimmered most beautifully. Removing the campu, he permitted her to examine it, and at once she noticed the delicately wrought figure of a bloodsucking tick, then another; and as her eyes followed the design she saw that the ticks were eating a heart. Chuquillanto asked him what this ornament was called, and he said it was called utusi.

The sun maiden gave him back his utusi and took leave of him, carrying with her a vivid memory of this ornament with its ticks so finely wrought that they seemed to be alive and, indeed, to be eating a heart, as we have said. All along the way she talked with her sister about the llama herder, and when they reached the palace, the door-keepers eyed them closely and examined them to see if they were carrying anything that might harm them. For it was well known that there were women in many parts of the country who carried love charms, small round tokens hidden by their lovers in the folds of their sashes or among the beads of their necklaces. Aware of this practice, the doorkeepers were on their guard and inspected the maidens carefully. At last they were allowed to enter the palace, where they were met by other sun women, who awaited them with all the greatest delicacies the land could provide, served in dishes of fine gold.

Chuquillanto did not care to eat. She went directly to

her chamber, saying only that she was tired, exhausted after her long walk. Her sister, however, ate with the other women, and if she had thoughts of Acoynapa, they did not seem to trouble her, though she did in fact let out an occasional sigh. But Chuquillanto had not a moment's peace. She had fallen deeply in love with the llama herder and was suffering all the more for not being able to express what she felt within her. She was a wise and sensible young woman, however, and so she lay down to rest and was soon fast asleep.

Now there were many richly appointed chambers in this great house of the Sun, and in these chambers lived the numerous sun women who had been brought from the four quarters of the Inca's realm: the northwest, the southwest, the northeast, and the southeast. And within the palace walls were four fountains of sweet, crystal-clear water, each of which flowed toward one of the four quarters, and in these fountains the women bathed, each in the one that ran toward the region from which she herself had been brought. The four fountains were named as follows: to the northwest flowed the fountain of pebbles, to the southwest the fountain of frogs, to the northeast the fountain of the water weed, to the southeast the fountain of algae.

Chuquillanto slept on, and as she slept she dreamed she saw a little night bird flying from tree to tree. As it flew and perched, it sang softly and sweetly. And when it had sung for a while, it came and rested in the folds of her skirt—in her lap—telling her not to be unhappy or to think of anything that would make her sad. She asked it if it could relieve her suffering, for she felt as though she would die, and the little bird agreed to do so, asking her to tell it why she suffered. Then she confessed her love for the keeper of the white llamas, whose name was Acoynapa, saying that she feared she might be killed unless she ran away with him. If she did not, and should she be found out by one of the women belonging to her Sun father, she would be put to death.

In reply the little night bird ordered her to rise from her bed and go out to the four fountains and sit among them and sing aloud whatever thought was uppermost in her mind. If the fountains approved, they would repeat her song, empowering her to do the thing she wished. So saying, the bird flew away. The sun maiden awoke. Fearfully and in great haste she put on her clothing; and as all the occupants of the palace were asleep, she was able to move about without being heard. She went at once to the four fountains, and placing herself among them, thinking only of the silver ornament with its heart consumed by ticks, she chanted:

> *Suck*
> *Tick*
> *Move*
> *Heart*
> *Come*

—and one after another the four fountains began to sing her song. They picked it up one by one, then they sang it in unison. Seeing that the fountains were favorable, the sun maiden withdrew. She rested comfortably during the remainder of the night, while the fountains murmured on.

As for the llama herder, when he returned to his hut he found that he could not stop thinking of the beautiful Chuquillanto. Troubled by his thoughts, he began to mourn. A new feeling had taken root in his innocent breast, causing him to long for love's fulfillment, and he took up his flute and began to play, so mournfully that the very rocks were moved to pity. At last, overwhelmed, he lost consciousness and fell to the ground. When he regained his senses, he wept many tears, crying, "Alas, alas for you! Sad, unhappy, unfortunate herdsman! The day of your death approaches, for there is no relief from this desire. Poor herdsman, what can you do? The only comfort is beyond reach, even out of sight." And with that he went inside his little hut. Exhausted by his suffering, he lay down to sleep.

Now in the village of Lares lived the llama herder's mother. She had been told by soothsayers that her son was desperately ill and that unless she could find a way to cure him he would die. Well aware of the cause of his misfortune, she obtained a wooden staff, which was most elegant and which, in a case such as this, could be very useful, and without stopping to rest she set out on the road toward the high country.

Being quick and agile, she reached the herdsman's hut before daybreak. Inside the hut she found her son unconscious, his face all wet with flowing tears. As he came to his senses and opened his eyes, he saw his mother and began moaning loudly. She consoled him as best she could, telling him not to despair and that she would have him cured within a few days.

She went outside then and among the crags began gathering nettles.* When she had collected a sufficient quantity, she prepared a nettle stew, which was not yet completely cooked, however, when the two sun maidens appeared. Chuquillanto had risen and dressed at dawn; as soon as it had come time to go walking among the green meadows of the high country, she had slipped out, accompanied by her sister, and come directly to Acoynapa's hut, for her heart allowed her to do nothing else.

When the maidens had reached the hut, they sat down by the doorway, tired from their journey. Noticing the old mother, they greeted her and asked if she could give them something to eat. The old woman knelt before them, explaining that she had only a nettle stew. But as soon as it was cooked, she served it to them and they ate with great relish.

Sadly Chuquillanto looked about her, discovering not a trace of the one she had hoped to find. The reason she did not see him is that the moment she and her sister had come into view the boy's mother had ordered him to put himself inside the wooden staff she had brought. And so the maiden assumed he had gone off with his llamas and did not even bother to ask where he might be. But seeing the staff, she commented on how pretty it was and asked the old woman where she had obtained it.

The old woman replied that the staff had formerly be-

* The prickly, itching nettles, to be eaten by Chuquillanto, will cure the hero's melancholy by causing his beloved to yearn for him irresistibly.

longed to one of the mistresses of the god Pachacamac, whose name was famous throughout the high country, and as an inheritance it had come down to her. No sooner had Chuquillanto heard this than she begged to have it, and so insistently that at last the old woman gave it to her. Taking it in her hands she found it even finer than she had thought at first, and after staying a while longer in the hut she took leave of the old woman and went off through the meadows, looking in all directions to see if her beloved herdsman might not appear.

We need make no special mention of the sister at this point, for she does not concern us. Rather, we speak only of Chuquillanto, who remained sad and pensive all along the way, watching for her herdsman, who did not appear. Greatly distressed, she continued on toward her palace. As usual, when she entered, the guards examined her closely, but seeing nothing new except for the staff, which was carried openly, they locked the doors behind her and were completely deceived.

The maidens proceeded to the inner rooms, where a splendid meal was set before them. When it had grown dark, everyone retired. Chuquillanto took her staff with her and placed it next to her bed, for this seemed to her the proper thing to do. As she lay down, thinking she was all alone, she began to cry, remembering the herdsman and the dream she had had the night before.

But her cares were short-lived, for already the staff had changed into its former self, and someone was calling her name: "Chuquillanto!" Startled, she arose and went to find a torch. Lighting it, she returned to her bed without making a sound, and there, kneeling before her, was the herdsman, shedding many tears. Shaken by the sight of him and satisfying herself that this indeed was he, she spoke to him, asking him how he had entered the palace. Then he told her about the staff, and Chuquillanto embraced him and covered him in her robes of fine compi cloth, patterned with the most exquisite designs. He slept with her then, but when dawn came he reentered the staff, and when he had concealed himself completely, and as soon as the daylight had spread over the land, his sun maiden and mistress set out once again from her father's palace.

Alone with her staff she roamed through the meadows, but in a mountain ravine she was together again with her beloved herdsman, who had changed back into his own self. It seems, however, that one of the guards had followed her. He discovered her in this hiding place, and seeing what had happened, he cried aloud. Chuquillanto and Acoynapa heard his cries and fled toward the mountains that rise above the town of Calca. Exhausted, they stopped to rest at the summit of a cliff, and there they fell asleep. But hearing great noises in their dreams, they rose up, she with one sandal held in her hand, the other still on her foot; and facing toward Calca, the two of them were turned into stone. The statues can still be seen from Calca and also from Haillabamba and from many other places as well, and I myself have seen them often. Those twin crags were called Pitusiray, and they are still so called to this day.

*Warrior from a painted plate of
the Mochica culture, north
coastal Peru*

A LATTER-DAY LEGEND

Utca Paucar

These things happened a long time ago, how long no one knows. Some say the story goes back to the days of the Inca empire. Others believe it is even older.

On the slopes of a great mountain stood the palace of an aged lord called Ahuapanti, ruler of a vast domain. Above the palace rose a mountain, crowned with snow; below ran the swift waters of a river, and across the river stretched endless hills, which in good times were covered with potato plantations and fields of corn.

Now this old lord was the father of a beautiful young woman called Yma Sumac, his only daughter, who enjoyed a secluded and most proper upbringing under the watchful care of her mother, whose name was Chimpu Huallca.

In those days it was the custom for youths and maidens to gather in the fields on nights of the full moon to scare away animals that might ruin the crops. There the young people would sing and dance to the sound of flutes and panpipes, and love would enter their hearts. But Yma Sumac could never be seen in the fields at such a late hour.

At harvest time the young men and women would meet again, and there would be singing and dancing to celebrate the bounty of the earth. But Yma Sumac would always remain in her father's palace.

She would allow herself to be seen only during the festivals of the guardian spirits, when no one could be excused from religious duties. But even on these occasions she did not participate in the dancing to the full extent that the others did, nor did she join in the merriment. With regard to the young men in particular, she was careful to keep her reserve.

In a neighboring province lived two brothers, Utca Paucar and Utca Mayta. The first was a soldier, the captain of his unit, famous for bravery and physical prowess; and the people told many stories about his deeds in war. The other brother was a farmer and herdsman. Though a fine-looking youth, he had no deeds. Yet his fields always produced a good harvest.

It happened that the first of these brothers met the

young daughter of Ahuapanti at one of the sacred festivals. He had the good fortune to share the cornmeal bread and the sacrificial meat with her, and afterward he held her precious hands as they danced the huayno. Her rare beauty and gentle manner immediately captivated the young warrior's heart. Determined to make her his wife, he began to frequent the house of her father, pretending he had come to hear tales of old-time warriors and to ask advice about leading troops to victory. Even so, he found it difficult to catch a glimpse of the one he desired and had to comfort himself with listening to the old man's stories.

Now Utca Mayta, at the same time, had also fallen in love with Ahuapanti's daughter. With no excuse for visiting the old lord, he would anxiously walk back and forth outside the palace walls. Although like his brother he had no chance to speak with the maiden, he saw her several times filling her jar at the fountain. But the fountain was close to the palace and no sooner would he draw near than she would disappear behind the walls, without having heard his call.

One day, as Utca Mayta was making his tour of the palace walls and Utca Paucar was just leaving after a conference with the old lord, the two brothers met. Obliged to explain themselves, they confessed their love for the maiden, and each admitted that he hoped to make her his wife. Neither felt that his love had been returned, yet neither would renounce his intentions in favor of the other. In order to avoid a quarrel, they decided to visit the father and lay their case before him. When they had done so, the old man, showing no preference, announced that he would marry his daughter to whichever of the brothers succeeded in diverting a particular stream that flowed down from the mountain, making the new channel pass directly in front of the palace gate.

The challenge posed by the old man was a difficult one, perhaps impossible, yet the rivals had no choice but to accept it.

Utca Paucar placed his hopes in his authority as a captain, for he was the commander of a large army. Summoning as many soldiers as he could, he lost no time in setting to work. As for Utca Mayta, he was able to muster only a handful of friends. But being a farmer, he had some experience in building aqueducts and had taken part in irrigation projects in the neighboring valleys. Consequently, he plotted the course of the new channel with greater skill than his rival, and in barely two months' time he had succeeded in bringing the waters down to the palace gate. Meanwhile, his brother, with all his soldiers, was not even halfway there.

Ahuapanti, keeping his word, prepared to grant his daughter to the winner. But Utca Paucar would not accept defeat, nor could he renounce his love for Yma Sumac. He felt he must have another chance, and at last he declared war on his brother.

Among the troops not all were in sympathy with Utca Paucar; many of the soldiers sided with his brother. The young men of the town were similarly divided; some joined the ranks of Utca Mayta, others took the part of his rival. Before long two powerful armies had been formed and a bloody struggle began. Fierce battles were waged in which first one side, then the other, would gain the upper hand, but with never a final victory. Days and months went by. A year passed and then another, and yet another. Still the fighting wore on, and still there was no conclusion. By this time there were few men left to sow the fields and few to tend them. The harvests were scanty and poor. The people began to go hungry. There were not enough supplies for the troops. At last, as the fighting let up and there came a time when famine threatened to put an end to the war, Utca Paucar challenged his brother to settle the dispute in single combat. Utca Mayta accepted.

As agreed, the two brothers met, each with a club in one hand and a shield in the other. But just as the contest was about to begin, Utca Paucar, who was larger and stronger than his opponent, realized that the match was unequal and that his conduct had been wrong. He laid down his weapon, admitted his error, and conceded the victory to his brother.

Utca Mayta and Yma Sumac were married in a solemn ceremony. All the local dignitaries, as well as those from neighboring provinces, were in attendance. Afterward there were many songs and dances and much to eat and drink. The celebration lasted for several days, as was the custom among our ancestors in those remote times.

But Utca Paucar was not present at the wedding. Overcome with grief, unable to end his suffering, he withdrew to a distant mountain, where he lived in misery for the rest of his days.

Design from a plaque possibly
representing the god Viracocha.
Tears of rain flow from the eyes

MYTHS OF ANCIENT PERU

Viracocha

At first there was only darkness, and within the darkness were the waters of the great lake, Titicaca. Then Viracocha, called Illa Ticsi Viracocha, *the Bright One, the First One, the Foam of the Sea,* came forth from the waters and made the earth and the sky. He created the first human beings. He disappeared, and still there was darkness.

But the first beings were displeasing to Viracocha and he emerged again from Lake Titicaca, and many like himself—many viracochas—were with him. He turned the first beings into stone, as punishment for the anger they had caused him. Then he created the sun and made it run in its proper course. Also, he created the moon and the stars, and he put them into the sky. This he did at Tiahuanaco.

And at Tiahuanaco he created new tribes of men, making each tribe from stone; and each tribe had its chieftain and its women who were pregnant and other women who had children on cradleboards. When the first tribe was finished, he set it aside there in Tiahuanaco, and he made another tribe and another. And on each of the figures he painted the dresses they were to wear, and those who were to wear their hair long were given long hair, and those who were to be shorn were shorn.

Then he summoned his viracochas and showed them all the tribes, telling them what each was to be named and where its home would be. He said: "As I have painted them and made them of stone, so shall they issue from fountains, rivers, caves, and rocks in the provinces that I have indicated to you."

Then he sent his viracochas toward the sunrise, ordering them to call forth the tribes. Two of them, however, he kept with him, sending one southwestward toward the seacoast and the other northeastward toward the forested lowlands; and these two then traveled north, calling forth more tribes. Viracocha himself went between them, taking the royal road to Cuzco and Cajamarca, and he too called forth tribes.

As he traveled along, he carried a staff. He was old, they say, and lean and bearded. His cloak was long and his hair was long.

When he reached the district of Cacha, where the Canas were to be, then he called forth the Cana tribe. But they came out armed, and when they saw Viracocha, not knowing him, they rushed upon him, weapons in hand, intending to kill him. Seeing them coming, he made fire fall from the sky and burned a mountain close to where they were. They saw the fire and were terrified. Then they threw down their weapons and ran toward Viracocha, casting themselves on the ground before him. When he saw them like this, he took up his staff and struck at the fire, and it died out.

Then he told them that he was their Creator, and they built him a great temple and offered much gold and silver.

Afterward he came to Urcos, where he climbed to the top of a high mountain. There he sat down and commanded the people who live in that place to emerge from the mountain. And because Viracocha sat down there, they built him a throne of gold.

From there he went on, calling forth the various tribes, until he reached Cuzco. In that place he brought forth the Alcahuizas, and he also named the site Cuzco; and he left instructions as to how the Incas were to be brought into being after his departure. Then he continued northward, calling forth the tribes.

At last he reached the seacoast in the district of Manta. And there, spreading his cloak, he moved on it over the waves and never reappeared, nor was he seen again. And because of the manner of his departure he was given the name Viracocha, *the Foam of the Sea*.

Coniraya and Cahuillaca

I

In the old days Coniraya Viracocha used to travel about
in human form, but as though he were very poor: his cloak
and his tunic were rags. Nobody recognized him. People
cried, "You louse-ridden wretch!"

Yet it was he who created all the villages. All the fields,
all the beautifully terraced hillsides: he spoke them into
existence with merely a word. It was he who taught the
use of aqueducts; and he made the water flow by letting

fall to the ground a single blossom of the reed called pupuna. As he went along, he made all sorts of things. And in his wisdom he disdained the other, local gods.

Now in those days, there was a woman called Cahuillaca. She too was a god, this Cahuillaca, and yet a virgin, though she was pretty. The gods and spirits all wanted to sleep with her; they desired her. But she would have none of them.

One day as this woman, whom no man could touch, sat weaving beneath an eggfruit tree, Coniraya, in his wisdom, changed himself into a bird and went and perched in the eggfruit tree. Placing his semen inside a ripe eggfruit, he let it fall beside the young woman. The woman was pleased and she ate it at once.

In this way and no other, they say, she grew pregnant, untouched by a man. And in nine months' time, just as all women give birth, so did she, though a virgin, give birth. Then for a year she nursed the child at her breast, asking "Whose little boy can this be?"

When the boy was a full year old, crawling on all fours, she summoned the gods and spirits to determine which of them might be the father. Hearing the summons, the gods were well pleased. They put on their good clothes and arrived, each thinking, "Only me will she love, only me."

They met at the place where she lived, called Anchicocha.

When all the gods and spirits were seated, the woman spoke: "You men, you lords, behold this child! Which of you gave him to me?" Then she asked each in turn, "Was it you? Was it you?" But no one answered "It was I."

Coniraya Viracocha sat at the very end—nothing but a

pauper. She scorned to question him, thinking, "How could my son be the child of this beggar?"

Inasmuch as so many lordly men were sitting there, and yet none would say "He is mine," she said at last to her little boy, "Go, find your father yourself!" Then she said to the gods, "Whichever of you is the father, the child will climb up on you."

Then the boy began at one end, crawling on all fours without stopping until he reached the other end, where his father sat. When he got there, he was filled with joy and crawled up at once on his father's thigh.

Seeing this, the mother flew into a rage, crying, "Can such a miserable wretch be my husband?" Then she picked up her child and ran in the direction of the sea.

"Now she will love me!" cried Coniraya Viracocha, and he threw on his robe of gold, terrifying the other gods. "Sister Cahuillaca, look! See how beautiful I am!" And as he rose up, the earth was suddenly bathed in light. But the goddess did not look back. She ran on, continuing her flight to the sea. Having given birth to the son of so hideous and crude a man, so she thought, she wished that she might disappear. Then she arrived at the Pachacamac Sea, where she and her son were changed to stone. They can still be seen there today: two rocks like human beings.

11

Far in the distance Coniraya pursued her, thinking each moment that she would appear and look back. He called out. He kept crying her name.

As he went along, he met a condor, and he asked it, "My brother, have you seen a woman?" The condor replied, "You will find her close by." Then the god spoke these words: "You shall live the longest of all the animals. When the guanaco dies, you alone shall eat its flesh, also the flesh of the vicuña and all the other game. If any man kills you, he himself shall be doomed to death."

Then he came to a skunk, and he asked her, "Sister, have you seen a woman?" She answered, "You will never find her. Already she is far away." Hearing this, he sentenced her severely, saying, "Because of what you tell me, you shall go about by night, not by day. Men shall scorn you, and you shall have an evil stench."

Then he met a puma, who told him, "She is close by, you will shortly overtake her." And the god answered, "You shall be venerated. You shall kill and eat the llama, especially the evil man's llama. Dancers shall wear your hide at sacred feasts and in this way you shall dance. They shall come to fetch you once a year, sacrificing llamas in your honor; and indeed you shall dance."

Then he met a fox. But the fox said, "She has gone far away, you will never find her." And the god answered, "As you travel along in the distance, men shall speak of you contemptuously, saying, 'There's a fox. The rascal!' And if someone kills you, he shall leave your pelt behind, for it shall be worthless."

Next he met a hawk. The hawk said, "She is yet close by. You will find her." Then the god replied, "You shall have much joy; and when you eat, your food shall be the hummingbird and other birds as well. And when you are killed, the man who has killed you shall honor you by sacrificing one of his llamas; when he dances, he shall place you upon his head so that you shall be his ornament."

Then he met some parrots. But the parrots said to him, "Already she is far away. You will see her no more." And Coniraya replied, "As you fly about, you shall screech. And as you look for your food, men shall hear your screeching and capture you with ease. You shall be miserable. You shall be despised."

And so he went on, predicting good fortune to whomever he met who would give him a good report. All others he cursed.

When he got to the seashore, he turned toward the place called Pachacamac, soon arriving at the home of the god Pachacamac's two unmarried daughters, who were guarded by a serpent.

Now, the mother of these two maidens had shortly beforehand gone out to the sea, looking for Cahuillaca; and the mother's name was She-Who-Gives-Birth-to-the-Dove. While she was out, Coniraya approached her elder daughter; he made her sleep with him. Then he tried to sleep with the younger one, too. But she changed herself into a dove and flew away. This, then, is why her mother was called She-Who-Gives-Birth-to-the-Dove.

Now, at that time, there was not even one little fish in the sea. She-Who-Gives-Birth-to-the-Dove kept them all in a very small tank in her home. Coniraya was angry, thinking, "Why has she gone to the shore, seeking this woman named Cahuillaca?" In his anger he threw the fish into the sea, and indeed the sea ever since has been teeming with fish. Then he left and went walking along the coast.

When She-Who-Gives-Birth-to-the-Dove returned, her daughter reported, "He slept with me!" Then, filled with anger, she set out to find him. She ran after him, calling his name, until finally he answered her, "Yes!" and waited.

Then she said to him, "Con, my dear, let me pick the lice from your hair." And so she loused him.

But as she was lousing him, she caused a great rock to spring up beside him, intending to tip it over and kill him. But Coniraya, in his wisdom, guessing what she had in mind, merely said, "I'll be back in a moment, dear sister. I have to urinate." And with that he escaped to the upland villages.

And here for a long while he remained and played pranks and made fun of many towns and many men.

The Macaw Woman

There came a time long ago when the earth was covered with water. As the water rose the people were drowned, all but two brothers, who fled to the mountain called Huaca-yñan. Still the water kept rising. It threatened to cover the mountain. But the mountain itself grew higher and higher, and in this way the brothers were saved.

When the flood had subsided and the land was dry, the brothers, nearly starved by now, came down from the mountain to look for food. All they could find were roots and a few herbs, barely enough to keep them alive.

Each day they would gather whatever they could. At night they would return exhausted to the little house they had built for themselves on the mountain.

One evening, as they entered the house, they were amazed to find cooked food to eat and chicha ready to drink. They couldn't imagine where it had come from or who might have brought it. Yet the next day the same thing happened. And on the following day it happened again. When this had gone on for ten days, the brothers decided to find out who their mysterious visitor might be.

The next day the elder brother remained at home. He hid in a corner and waited. Presently two birds arrived, bringing food. They were macaws, yet they had human faces and wore their hair fastened in front the way women still do even now. As soon as they came into the house, the larger of the two removed her mantle. The young man could see that they were beautiful. As they began to prepare the food they had brought, he rushed forth and tried to seize them. Enraged, they flew off, leaving nothing to eat.

When the younger brother returned and found that no food had been cooked as on previous days, he asked what had happened. His brother told him about the macaws, how he had tried to capture them, and how they had flown away. Then both brothers were very troubled.

The next day the younger brother decided that he too would remain in hiding, and together the young men waited to see if the macaws would return. Finally, at the end of three days, the birds reappeared and began to prepare food as before. The brothers watched carefully. As soon as the food was cooked, they jumped up and shut the door with the two macaws inside. The birds were furious, they tried to escape, but only the larger of the two succeeded. The brothers seized the smaller bird and, grasping her tightly, would not let her go.

The smaller macaw then became their wife, and in time she gave birth to six sons and daughters. For many years they lived on the mountain, planting the seeds the macaw woman had brought and gathering the harvests.

We are all descended, they say, from these six sons and daughters. We are all children of the macaw. And for this reason the mountain Huaca-yñan is a holy mountain. The macaw, too, is holy; and its feathers are worn at sacred feasts.

*Double-serpent motif from a wall
in the ancient city of Chanchán,
north coastal Peru*

MYTHS THAT HAVE
SURVIVED

The Serpents

There was once a time when the Valley of Jauja, where the Mantaro River now flows, was covered by the waters of an enormous lake. In the middle of this lake there lived a serpent.

At first the serpent was all alone. But in time the rainbow created a second serpent to keep the first one company. It was not quite so large and also considerably darker than the first, which, when fully grown, was of a whitish color. But the two became enemies and soon were fighting for control of the lake. Their struggles were violent, and often the lake would be churned into great columns of water, upon which the larger serpent would rise far into the sky. Once, as it swooped down upon the smaller one, it attacked with such fury that it lost a huge piece of its tail.

Angered by these disturbances, the god Ticsi sent a thunderstorm. Both serpents were struck dead by lightning. As they sank back into the swollen lake, it broke free at its southern rim and all the water came pouring out.

When the valley had been formed in this manner, then the first two human beings, called Mama and Taita, were hurled forth from a spring. Until then they had remained hidden in the earth for fear of the serpents. In later days the descendants of this pair constructed the temple of Huarivilca, the ruins of which can still be seen.

Today it is widely believed that the serpents still live in a cave, where from time to time they grow to enormous size. And taking advantage of the winds that blow up during thunderstorms, they try to ride into the sky. But they are always killed by lightning striking down through the clouds. And when a serpent appears in the sky, if it is white, the year will be good; if it is black, the year will be bad.

The Condor Seeks a Wife

A condor fell in love with a young woman tending her flock of sheep. He changed himself into a handsome young man and came and stood beside her where her flock was grazing.

"What do you do here?" he said.

"I graze my flock," she answered. "I sing my songs, and with my slingshot I chase away the fox who comes to eat my lambs and the great condor who tries to snatch me up in his talons."

"Would you like me to stay with you and help you chase the fox and scare away the condor?"

"Oh no," she replied, "for then I would lose my freedom. I love my sheep and I love to be free, to be alone, and to sing. I do not wish to marry."

"Then I will go. But you have not seen the last of me."

The next day the condor returned, again disguised as a young man.

"We can talk, can't we?" he said.

"Yes, we can talk," she said. "Tell me, where do you come from?"

"I come from the high mountaintops, close to the thunder," he said. "I see the first light of dawn and the last light of evening. And there among the brilliant snows I enjoy pure solitude and perfect silence. Won't you go there with me? You would be the queen of the air. The clear blue sky would be our roof, and from deep in the valley the flowers would send up their perfume. Won't you go there, my love?"

"No, I do not care for your mountaintops. I prefer my pasture and my sheep. And I love my mother. She would cry for me if I were gone."

"I will say no more," he said. "But do me one small favor. I have a burning itch behind my shoulder. Lend me the long pin from your shawl so I can scratch it."

The young woman lent him the pin, and when he had finished using it he went away.

The next day this same young man returned.

"You have bewitched me," he said, "and I cannot live without you. Come away with me now."

"No, I must not," she said. "My sheep would miss me. My mother would weep."

"Ah," he said suddenly, "I have the same burning itch behind my shoulder. If only you would rub it for me with your smooth fingers—smooth as alpaca wool—you would cure me forever."

As he bent over, the incautious young woman climbed onto his back. The moment he felt her resting on his shoulders he became a condor and flew swiftly into the sky with his precious cargo between his wings.

Higher and higher they rose, and after a soaring voyage they reached a cave near the summit of a mountain. In that cave lived the condor's mother, an ancient lady with faded plumage. And in other caves on the same peak lived other condors. A great multitude.

The condors greeted the young woman's arrival with shouts of joy and noisy flappings of their wings. The old mother was delighted to see her and anxiously cradled her in her huge wings, for she was shivering in the cold air.

The girl was happy with her young condor. He was affectionate.

But he brought her nothing to eat.

At last she said to him, "Your tender caresses make my heart happy. But I am growing weak with hunger. Don't forget that I must eat and drink. I need fire. I need meat. I need the good things that grow in the earth. I am hungry, my love, and thirsty."

The condor took flight. Discovering an untended kitchen, he stole some hot coals from the hearth and carried them home. With his beak he opened a spring in the mountainside and brought forth clear water. From the fields and pathways far below he collected bits of flesh from dead animals. He dug up gardens and brought home potatoes.

The meat was foul-smelling. The potatoes had gone soft. Nearly overcome with hunger, the young woman nevertheless devoured this unpleasant food.

She wished for bread, but the condor was unable to provide it.

All this while the young woman's mother was weeping in her empty house. The young woman herself began to feel homesick. She wearied of the bad food and the constant embraces of her amorous condor. She began to be thin and her body grew feathers. She laid eggs. She was indeed the condor's wife, the queen of the air. Hers was the work of hatching chicks that would someday soar fearlessly through the sky like their father.

And still her abandoned mother wept inconsolably in her house. Pitying her, a parrot who lived in the neighborhood came and spoke to her:

"Do not weep, dear woman. Your daughter is alive in the high mountains. She is the wife of the great condor. But if you will give me the corn in your garden and enough room in your trees to perch and nest, I will bring her back to you."

The mother accepted this offer. She gave the parrot her corn patch and room to nest in her trees.

The parrot flew to the high mountaintop. He chose a moment when the condors were off guard and picked up the young woman and carried her back to her mother's side. She was thin and ill-smelling from the poor food she had eaten. The glossy feathers that hung about her gave her the ridiculous air of an outcast human dressed up like a bird. But her mother received her gladly. She washed her body with the tears from her eyes. She dressed her in the finest clothes she had. Then she held her in her lap and gazed at her with boundless satisfaction.

Bereaved and angry over the loss he had suffered, the condor set out in search of the parrot. He found him in the garden, stuffed with corn, flitting contentedly from tree to tree.

He swooped down on the parrot and devoured him whole. But the parrot went straight through the condor's body and came out the other end. The condor swallowed him again, and again he came out. Furious, the condor seized the parrot, tore him to pieces with his sharp talons, and swallowed him piece by piece. But for each piece he swallowed, a pretty little parrot came out the other end. And this, they say, is the origin of the parrots we know today.

The sorrowful condor returned to his mountain. He dyed his plumage black as a sign of mourning. And the tears he left behind became the airborne ashes that swirl like butterflies above the hearth.

The Rainbow

When the sun comes up and a mist is in the air and the whole sky is brilliant, then from a natural fountain the rainbow is born, stretching forth in an enormous arc.

But it fears the people on earth; their faces are much too lively, and it draws itself back through the sky like a braided rope of many colors.

There were once some little boys who set out to find its feet. But its toes are made of crystal and it always hides them. So the little boys were unable to find what they were looking for and they threw stones at the rainbow.

When the rainbow enters the body of a man or woman, then the person becomes gravely ill. But the sick person will be cured if he unravels a ball of yarn made of seven colors.

The Boy Who
Rose to the Sky

There once lived a man and a woman who had an only
son. The man grew wonderful potatoes in a plot that was
far from the house. They were luxuriant, and he alone
had the seed to grow them. But at night thieves would
come and tear up the plants and steal the potatoes. And
so at last the father and mother called their young man
and said to him, "Why should thieves carry off all our
potatoes when we have a strong young man like you?
Go out and stand guard. Sleep next to the garden and
you'll catch the thieves."

The boy set off to look after the garden. Three nights went by. The first night the boy remained awake, watching the potatoes without sleeping. But at daybreak sleep overcame him and he nodded. At that moment the thieves came into the garden and dug up the potatoes. Disappointed, he returned to his parents' house and told them what had happened. When they had heard his story, they said, "We forgive you this time. Go back and watch more carefully."

The boy went back. He watched the garden until daybreak, his eyes wide open. Just at midnight, however, he blinked for a moment. And during that moment the thieves slipped into the garden. The boy opened his eyes and kept on watching till dawn. He saw no thieves. But in the morning he had to go back to his parents and tell them, once more, that the potatoes had been stolen.

He said to them, "I stood guard the whole night through. But the thieves came at midnight just as I blinked my eyes."

Hearing this, his parents replied, "What? You expect us to believe you were robbed before your very eyes? You were off chasing girls, no doubt, and having a good time." And with that they beat him and scolded him endlessly.

The next day they sent him back to the garden, still sore from his beating. "Now you'll know what we mean when we tell you to stand guard," they said.

The boy returned to his task, and from the moment he arrived at the edge of the field he watched attentively, without making a move. That night the moon shone brightly. He kept watch until dawn, his eyes fixed on the potato field. And yet, as he watched, his eyelids trembled, and for a moment he slept. In that instant of sleep, in that twinkling, a swarm of beautiful princesses—dazzling little maidens—came and filled the garden. Their faces were like flowers, their hair shone like gold, they were dressed in silver. With great haste, all working together, they began to dig the potatoes. Though they seemed to be princesses, they were in fact the stars come down from the sky.

Just then the boy opened his eyes, gazed at the garden, and exclaimed, "Such beautiful creatures. If only I could catch them. Yet how can they be so lovely and shining and stoop to such work as this?"

As he spoke, his love-struck heart nearly burst. Then he thought to himself, "Perhaps I could keep just two of them for myself." And he leaped toward the beautiful thieves. But only at the last moment and with great difficulty was he able to seize merely one of them. The others rose into the sky and disappeared like fading lights.

Then to the one star he had been able to catch he said angrily, "Why were you stealing from my father's garden?" And with that he led her to the little hut that stood beside the field. He spoke no more about the theft, but said, "Stay with me and be my wife."

The maiden refused. She was frightened, and pleaded with the boy: "Let me go! Let me go! Have mercy! Don't you know that my sisters will tell my parents about this? I'll give back all the potatoes we've stolen from you. Don't force me to live on earth!"

The young man paid no heed to her protests. Again he seized her. But he did not return to his parents' house. In-

Myths That Have Survived

stead, he and the star maiden remained in the little hut.

Meanwhile, his parents were thinking, "The thieves have stolen more potatoes from that worthless boy. What other reason can there be that he doesn't come home?" It was getting late. The mother decided to bring some food to him out at the garden and see for herself.

From inside the hut, the boy and the girl were watching the path. When they saw the mother, the girl said to the boy, "Neither your father nor your mother must ever see me."

Then the boy ran out to meet his mother and called to her, "No, Mother! Don't come near. Wait for me there! Back there!"

He took the food from her in back of the hut and brought it in to the princess. The mother, as soon as she'd delivered the food, turned around and went home. Then she said to her husband, "Our son has caught a potato thief, a girl come down from the sky, and now he's keeping her in the little hut. He says he will marry her. But he won't let a soul come near."

Meanwhile, the boy, thinking to deceive the maiden, said, "Now that it's night, we must go to my house."

But the princess insisted, "Your parents must not see me. I can never meet them."

But the young man lied to her, saying, "I have my own house." And in the dark he led her along the path.

So against her will he succeeded in bringing her home, and he showed her to his parents. They were astonished at the sight of this radiant creature, so beautiful that words cannot describe her.

They kept her and took care of her and loved her dearly. But they did not allow her to go out. No one ever met her or saw her.

Now it happened that when the princess had lived with the young man's parents for a long time she became pregnant and gave birth to a child. But the child died mysteriously, without anyone knowing why.

As for the princess's shining garments, they kept them hidden away. They dressed her in everyday clothes, and so she lived on in this way with the boy and his parents.

But one day the boy went off a great distance to do some work. When he had left, the girl was able to slip outside, acting as though she were not going far. But in fact she returned to the sky.

The boy came back to the house. He asked for his wife, but couldn't find her. And when he knew she had disappeared, he burst into tears.

They say that he wandered out into the mountains and went everywhere, weeping crazily, walking on in his sleep, entranced. And on one of the desolate peaks he came to a sacred condor, and the condor said to him, "Young man, why do you weep like this?"

Then the boy told him all that had happened. "And so you see, my lord, this most beautiful woman was mine. But I have no idea which path she has taken. I am lost. And I fear she has gone back up to the sky."

When he had finished, the condor replied, "Don't cry, young man. It is true; she has returned to the heavens. But if you wish, and if your misery is so great, then I will carry you up to that world. All I ask is that you bring me two llamas. One to eat here, and one to eat on the way."

"Very well, my lord," said the boy. "I will bring the two llamas you have asked for. I beg you to wait for me here."

Without delay he set off for home to fetch the llamas. When he reached the house, he said to his parents, "Mother, Father! I'm going to get my wife. I've found someone who will take me to where she is. All he asks is two llamas, and I'm going to bring them to him now."

So he brought the two llamas to the condor. Immediately the condor took one of them and devoured it down to the bare bones, tearing off the flesh with his beak. He made the young man slit the throat of the other one so he could have it to eat on the way. Then he had the boy throw the carcass over his shoulders and stand on a rock. As he picked him up, he gave him this warning:

"You must close your eyes and keep them shut. Don't open them for any reason. And every time I say to you 'Meat!' you must put a piece of the llama into my beak."

Then the condor took flight.

The boy obeyed and never opened his eyes even for an instant. He kept his eyelids tightly shut. "Meat!" the condor would say, and the boy would cut off large pieces of llama and put them into the condor's beak. But in the course of this soaring voyage, the meat ran out.

Before they had left the ground, the condor had warned the young man, "If when I say 'Meat!' you do not put meat in my beak, I will drop you no matter where we are." And so, out of fear, the boy began to cut pieces of flesh from the calf of his leg. Each time the condor would ask for meat, he would give him a tiny portion. And so, at the cost of his own flesh, he succeeded in having the condor carry him up to the sky. And they say it took a year to reach such a great height.

When they got there, the condor rested awhile. Then he lifted the boy again and flew with him to the shore of a distant lake. Then he said to the boy, "Now, my dear, you must bathe in this lake."

The boy bathed himself at once. And the condor also bathed.

When they arrived in the sky, they were dirty and bearded. They had grown old. But when they came out of the water they were handsome and young. Then the condor said to the boy:

"Before us, on the other side of this lake, is a great temple. A ceremony is to be held there soon. Go and wait at the door. The sky maidens will come to attend the ceremony; they will come in great numbers, and all their faces will be just like the face of your wife. As they pass in front of you, you must keep perfectly still. The one who belongs to you will be the last to come; she will brush against you. Then you must seize her and not let her go."

The young man did as the condor told him. He came to the door of the great temple and waited. Soon a host of young women arrived, all exactly alike. One after another they went inside, glancing at the boy with expressionless faces. It would have been impossible to tell which one was his wife. But just as the last few were passing by, one of them brushed against him with her arm. Then she too entered the temple.

It was the shining temple of the Sun and the Moon, the father and mother of all the stars. It was the place where the sky people gathered; and all the stars came there each day to worship the Sun. And they sang, making beautiful music for the Sun. The stars were innumerable white maidens; they were princesses.

When the ceremony was over, they began to leave. The boy was still waiting beside the door. They glanced at him with the same expressionless faces. And again it was impossible to tell which one was his wife. Just as before, one of the princesses touched him with her arm. Then she tried to run away. But he caught her and would not let her go.

She led him toward her house, saying, "Why are you here? I was going to come back to you."

When they got to the house, the boy was quite cold, for he had had nothing to eat. The young woman knew he was hungry and said, "Take this bit of quinoa and cook it." And she gave him a scant spoonful of quinoa grain. The boy was watching closely, however, and he saw where she kept the quinoa. When he noticed how little she had offered him, he thought to himself, "What a small portion! How can this fill me up when I've had nothing to eat for a year?"

Then the young woman said, "I have to go to my parents for a moment. They mustn't see you. But while I'm gone, make a soup from the quinoa I've given you."

When she left, the boy got up and went to the place where the quinoa was kept, helped himself to a good-sized portion, and threw it into the pot. Immediately the soup rose up in a boil and came gushing forth. He ate as much as he could, filling himself till he could eat no more. Then he buried the rest. But even so, it continued to swell.

Just then the princess returned, and she said to him, "This is no way to eat our quinoa! Why did you increase the portion I gave you?"

Then she helped the boy get rid of the overflowing quinoa so that her parents would not discover it. She warned him, "My parents must never see you. You must hide."

And so he remained hidden, and the beautiful star brought food to his hiding place.

For a year the young man lived with his wife in this manner. But when the year had passed, she began to neglect him and no longer brought him his food. One day she went out, saying, "The time has come when you must leave." After that she did not come back to the house. She had abandoned him at last.

Then the boy's eyes filled with tears and he returned to the edge of the sky lake. When he got there, he saw the condor rising up in the distance. As he ran to meet him, the condor flew to his side, and he saw that the sacred condor had grown old. And the condor could see that the boy, too, had grown old and wrinkled. As they met, they both cried out at once, "How have things been with you?"

Then the young man told him all that had happened

and said, "Aye, my lord, it is sad. My wife has abandoned me. She has gone away forever."

The condor lamented the young man's fate. "How could it all have turned out like this? Poor friend!" he said. Then he came close and stroked him gently with his wings.

As before, the young man begged the condor, "My lord, lend me your wings. Take me back to earth to my parents' house."

And the condor replied, "Very well. I will take you. But first we must bathe in the lake."

Then they both bathed and were made young.

When they had come out of the water, the condor said to him, "If I carry you, you must give me two more llamas."

"My lord, I will give you the two llamas when I get back to my house."

The condor was willing. Then he took the boy on his wings and set off. The flight to earth lasted a year, and when it was over the boy fulfilled his promise and gave the condor two llamas.

Then the boy went into the house and greeted his parents. They were old, very old. They were grieving and there were tears in their eyes. The condor said to them, "I have brought back your son, safe and sound. Now you must care for him lovingly."

And the young man said to his parents, "Dear Father, dear Mother, there is no other woman I can love. Never again will I find a wife like the one I have lost. I will remain unmarried till the day I die."

And his old parents answered him, "Very well, my son, you may do as you choose. If you do not wish to marry, we will take care of you ourselves."

And so, with a heavy heart, he lived on.

And mine too is a heart that has loved. I too have suffered much and wandered far.

I feel the tears come into my eyes.

*Moths from a painted vase of
the Inca period*

MODERN FABLES AND
ANIMAL TALES

The Moth

A man and a woman lived happily together with their only child, a little boy.

But the man went off on a journey, leaving his wife in tears, and while he was away she spent the nights sleeplessly spinning.

One night, as the little boy lay awake, he asked his mother, "What is that that flutters there beside you, that I hear you talking to?" The mother answered, "Oh, just someone who loves me, a little friend who comes and keeps me company."

When the man returned from his journey, his wife was out of the house. He began talking with his little boy, asking him how his mother had spent the nights while he was gone. "Someone who loves her came every night," said the little boy, "and she stayed up very late, spinning and talking to him."

Hearing this, the man went out to find his wife. When he found her, he threw her over a cliff and killed her.

Then one night, as he sat quietly before the fire, thinking of what had happened, his little boy cried out, "There he is, Mama's lover! The one who came and kept her company!" and he pointed to the moth that had come to his mother's side during the long nights of her husband's absence. Realizing his mistake, the man sank into a deep despair. His grief overwhelmed him, he no longer moved, and at last he was dead.

Why the Fox
Has a Huge Mouth

One day many years ago, at a time when his mouth was
still small and dainty, as in fact it used to be, the fox was
out walking and happened to notice a huaychao singing
on a hilltop. Fascinated by the bird's flute-like bill, he
said politely, "What a lovely flute, friend Huaychao, and
how well you play it! Could you let me try it? I'll give
it back in a moment, I promise."

The bird refused. But the fox was so insistent that at
last the huaychao lent him its bill, advising him to sew

up his lips except for a tiny opening so that the "flute" would fit just right.

Then the fox began to play. He played on and on without stopping. After a while the huaychao asked for its bill back, but still the fox kept on. The bird reminded him, "You promised. Besides, I only use it from time to time; you're playing it constantly." But the fox paid no attention and kept right on.

Awakened by the sound of the flute, skunks came out of their burrows and climbed up the hill in a bustling throng. When they saw the fox playing, they began to dance.

At the sight of the dancing skunks, the fox burst out laughing. As he laughed, his lips became unstitched. His mouth tore open and kept on tearing until he was grinning from ear to ear. Before the fox could regain his composure, the huaychao had picked up its bill and flown away.

To this day the fox has a huge mouth—as punishment for breaking his promise.

The Dancing Fox

Foxes love to dance. They dance in the dark with young women who slip quietly from their beds and come running out into the night.

But the fox who dances must wear a disguise. He must hide his long, bushy tail. He must wrap it around him and stuff it inside his trousers, though when he does he is really too warm. He perspires. Yet still he is able to dance.

Now, one of these foxes was young and amorous, and he never missed the nightly dancing. Toward morning, however, as the cock began to crow, he would always hurry away.

This fine fox was a subtle flatterer, a favorite with all the young women. Each of them wanted to dance with him. And as it happened, one or another would sometimes feel slighted and grow resentful.

One of them once, in a fit of pique, drew her companions aside and pointed out that the fox always left before dawn. Who was he? And why did he run away?

The young women wondered. Then they made up their minds to catch him and hold him until it was daylight.

The next night, when it was fully dark, they made their circle and began to dance. Soon the fox appeared, as usual disguised as a young man in shirt and trousers. Suspecting nothing, he danced and sang. The girls made him heady with their caresses, and he became more spirited and more flattering than ever.

As soon as the cock crowed, he started to leave. "No, no," they all cried, "don't go! Not yet! The cock crows six times. You can stay till the fifth."

The dancing continued, and there were more caresses. The fox forgot that he had to leave, and at last the white light of dawn appeared. Frightened, he tried to flee. But the young women held him. They entangled him in their arms. Then suddenly, with a growl, he bit their hands, leaped over their heads, and ran.

As he leaped, his trousers ripped open and out flew his tail. The girls all shrieked with laughter. They called after him and mocked him as he ran out of sight, his long, bushy tail waving between his legs. Then he disappeared and was seen no more. He never came back again.

The Mouse Husband

A mouse fell in love with a pretty young woman and
changed himself into a slender young man, quite long-
faced, however, and with tiny, bright eyes. He spoke with
a thin, whistling voice, and his manners were excellent.
He was always seemly, always pleasant. But he would
grow frightened and disappear whenever he heard his
mother-in-law coming, for she had the face of a cat.

"I'm off, I'm off!" he would say. "They're calling me!
I have to go back!" And with that he would run and hide.

The young woman returned his love, and it happened

that in nine months' time she gave birth to a tiny little boy with a voice so shrill that it was a pleasure just to hear him squeaking away.

The mouse husband was exceedingly fond of his beloved, and he filled the bins of her storeroom with good things to eat that he stole from neighboring farms. She had everything she wanted. "I want corn," she would say; and during the night her husband, aided by countless numbers of his fellow mice, would carry home corn for his wife.

But it made the young woman uneasy that her husband would not stay with her. At the approach of her mother he would always flee, for indeed her face was that of a cat, and he, of course, was merely a mouse disguised as a man.

One day he decided to reveal his secret, and he called to his wife, "Come! I'm out here!"

The young woman stepped outside, holding her baby in her arms. But looking about her, she saw no one at all. She sat down to wait, placing her baby next to the wall. From out of a hole came a mouse. It crawled over the child as it lay on the ground, turned around, and crawled over it again, caressing it with its tail and licking its little face. Then it kissed it on its tiny lips and disappeared.

Tired of waiting, still wondering where her husband might be, the young woman went back inside and said to her old mother, "He made me come for nothing. I waited. I looked for him. But I couldn't find him. There was only a mouse that came out of its hole and crawled back and forth over my little boy. It caressed him with its tail, kissed him on his tender little mouth, and ran away."

The mother flew into a rage and scolded her furiously. "So you married a mouse! I knew it myself by his shrill little voice!" And in a fit of anger she clawed the little baby, crushed it, and strangled it before the young woman could rush to its aid.

When her husband came in, she said to him, "Where were you? I looked for you. No one was there but a mouse."

"Young woman, young woman!" he cried. "That mouse was I, your lover, your lord!"

Then the young woman told him how her mother had discovered his secret and killed the child.

Grief-stricken, the mouse picked up his dead son, wept over him, and carried him far, far away. He buried him beneath a cantuta plant that he watered again and again with his tears so it would always flourish and never wither.

After that he went home to wreak his revenge. He called his mouse fellows together and told them of his misfortune. He asked them to help him, and they all went into the house in a pack and emptied the bins of the food they had previously brought. When nothing was left, they surrounded the old mother, toppled her to the floor, and gnawed her flesh. They ate her up, leaving nothing but a skeleton, and then they ran off, and they never came back again.

The Grateful Dove

Once there were two bad boys, who liked to torture animals. They hated to work in the vegetable patch, and they did not care to do chores for their old parents. They wanted to do no work at all. One day they ran away from home, bringing along their little brother, whom they had tricked with false promises.

They ran quickly, fearing they might be overtaken. Much to their annoyance, however, they had to keep stopping for the little one, who was slow and kept falling behind.

But at last they too were tired. And with no place to go, their food used up, hungry and quite lost on the high plains, they lay down to rest.

Overcome with remorse at having allowed himself to be tricked, Lanchi—for that was the name of the little brother—fell into a deep sleep.

As he slept, the other two plotted how best to get rid of him. He had eaten their food and was constantly whining to go home. Besides, the time had come for them to carry out their plan. How should they do it?

One of the brothers was worse than the other. "Let's kill him," he said, "because then he won't talk and we can be sure they'll never find us." But the other, whose name was Yahuar, said, "No, it would be better to pluck out his eyeballs. Then we can eat them."

They couldn't make up their minds. Suddenly Yahuar, quick as a streak, swooped down and clamped his knee against the little boy's neck, holding him fast. Now wide awake, the boy struggled to get free. But this only made his brother furious, and he choked him still harder.

The poor child's face was flushed and contorted, and his lips grew purplish. His breath came in short gasps as he tried desperately to keep from suffocating. Terror-stricken, he lay helpless, his eyes bulging.

Then the other brother, grim-faced, leaped toward him with arching fingers, and like a vulture who pecks out the eyes of a lamb held fast between his claws, he seized the eyes of the little boy, twisted them, tore them loose from their sockets, and jerked them out.

The two were crueler than jaguars. They paid no heed to their victim's piteous screams, nor were they disturbed by the horrible spectacle of what they had done. Crazed with bloodthirst, like hungry beasts, they gobbled up the still-gazing eyeballs, as if to destroy the last, reflected image of their atrocious crime.

Wordless and without remorse, the two monsters abruptly withdrew, pursued only by their gloomy shadows.

The poor little boy, overwhelmed by his suffering, made not a sound. He lay perfectly still, his empty sockets drawn shut with pain, his face covered with the blood that kept seeping out like spring water from cracks in a rock.

But at last the deathly silence was broken by a melodious voice that soothed his pain, singing:

"*Urpái . . . cucúy . . . tanrán!*
Urpái . . . cucúy . . . tanrán!"

Blind and forsaken, the little boy raised himself up and, stumbling as he tried to walk, directed his steps toward the soothing voice. It was the voice of a dove. Presently he bumped against a quenual tree, and it was from the upper branches of this tree that the song seemed to come. Happily he embraced the quenual, climbed it, and seized the dove in its nest.

The captured dove, sobbing, begged to be released: "What harm have I done you? You humans are cruel! You murder your own brothers! Let me go, and I will soothe your pain with my cooing:

"Urpái . . . cucúy . . . tanrán!
Urpái . . . cucúy . . . tanrán!"

Touched by pity, the little boy set the dove free, but pleaded with it to guide him to food and drink.

Scarcely able to believe that there could be a human with compassion in its heart, let alone a child, the little dove, in return, offered the boy a healing white powder to sprinkle on his wounds, gave him two round crystals to fill his empty sockets, and instructed him to tap them gently each day with a little stick.

The boy did as he was told, and little by little the dark became light. And at last he saw the sun that hangs in the sky and lights the world.

Filled with gratitude, he dropped to his knees and threw his hands up. What could he do for the dove?

"You may take me with you," said the dove. "But do not take away my freedom. And each day at dawn, as the morning star begins to fade, you will hear me call:

"Urpái . . . cucúy . . . tanrán!
Urpái . . . cucúy . . . tanrán!"

Notes on Sources

Apu Inca Atahuallpaman (page ix). Freely translated from J. M. B. Farfán, "Poesía folklórica quechua," *Revista del Instituto de Antropología de la Universidad Nacional de Tucumán*, Vol. 2, no. 12, Tucumán, Argentina, 1942, pp. 543 ff. (The entire poem runs to sixty-nine lines.) I have compared the Spanish versions in José María Arguedas and Francisco Carrillo, *Poesía y Prosa Quechua* (Lima, 1967), and in Jesús Lara, *La Literatura de los Quechuas* (La Paz, 1969).

The Rod of Gold (page 27). Freely translated from Garcilaso de la Vega, *Comentarios reales de los Incas,* Lib. I, cap. 15–17.

Mayta Capac (page 33). Translated, with omissions, from Pedro Sarmiento de Gamboa, *Historia de los Incas,* cap. 16–17.

The Storm (page 37). Translated from Francisco de Avila, "Tratado y relación de los errores, falsos Dioses, y otras supersticiones . . . de Huarocheri . . ." cap. 23. For my translations from Avila's manuscript I am indebted to the edition of Hermann Trimborn and Antje Kelm, entitled *Francisco de Avila* (Gebr. Mann Verlag: Berlin, 1967).

The Vanishing Bride (page 42). Translated from Avila, op. cit., cap. 14. See note for "The Storm," immediately preceding.

A Messenger in Black (page 45). Adapted from Juan de Santacruz Pachacuti Yamqui Salcamaygua, *Relación de antigüedades deste reino del Perú.* The section concerning Huayna Capac is to be found about four fifths of the way through this relatively brief chronicle.

The Oracle at Huamachuco (page 47). Translated from Sarmiento de Gamboa, op. cit., cap. 64.

The Llama Herder and the Daughter of the Sun (page 49). Translated, with omissions, from Martín de Morúa, *Historia del origen y genealogía real de los Reyes Incas del Perú.* I have used the edition of Constantino Bayle (Madrid, 1946), also the more heavily edited versions of Jesús Lara (*Leyendas Quechuas,* Buenos Aires, 1960) and Jorge Basadre (*Literatura Inca,* Paris, 1938).

Utca Paucar (page 61). Freely translated from Lara, *Leyendas Quechuas.*

Viracocha (page 69). Adapted from Juan de Betanzos, *Suma y narración de los Incas,* cap. 1–2, with additional details supplied from Pedro de Cieza de León, *Segunda parte de la crónica del Perú,* Lib. II, cap. 5; from Cristóbal de Molina, *Fábulas y ritos de los Incas;* and from Santacruz Pachacuti, op. cit.

Coniraya and Cahuillaca (page 72). Translated from Avila, op. cit., cap. 2. See note for "The Storm," above.

The Macaw Woman (page 78). Adapted from Molina, op. cit. The myth of the macaw woman is to be found in the opening pages of Molina's work.

The Serpents (page 85). Adapted from José María Arguedas and Francisco Izquierdo Ríos, *Mitos, leyendas y cuentos peruanos,* [Lima, 1947], pp. 65–6.

The Condor Seeks a Wife (page 87). Translated, with omissions, from M. Rigoberto Paredes, *El Arte Folkórico de Bolivia,* 2nd ed., La Paz, [1949], pp. 65–7.

The Rainbow (page 92). Translated, with omissions, from "El Turmanye" in Arturo Jiménez Borja, *Cuentos Peruanos,* Lima [1937].

The Boy Who Rose to the Sky (page 94). Freely translated from José María Arguedas, *Canciones y Cuentos del Pueblo Quechua,* Lima, 1949, pp. 105–14.

The Moth (page 109). Freely translated from Arguedas and Carrillo, op. cit., pp. 78–9.

Why the Fox Has a Huge Mouth (page 111). Adapted from "El Zorro y el Huaychao" in Borja, op. cit.

The Dancing Fox (page 113). Freely translated from Paredes, op. cit., pp. 69–70.

The Mouse Husband (page 115). Translated from Paredes, op. cit., pp. 68–9.

The Grateful Dove (page 118). Freely translated from Arguedas and Carrillo, op. cit., pp. 89–91.

Glossary of Indian Terms

ALPACA | Wool-bearing member of the camel family, closely related to the llama.

CAMPU | Name of a silver ornament mentioned in "The Llama Herder and the Daughter of the Sun."

CANTUTA | An evergreen shrub (*Cantua buxifolia*) with red-and-yellow flowers, member of the phlox family. It is the national flower of Peru.

CHICHA | A native beer made of fermented corn.

COMPI | A superior type of cloth, finished on both sides, usually woven with threads of various colors.

CONDOR | An enormous vulture with a wing span of ten feet or more.

COYA | The Inca's wife, the queen.

GUANACO | Member of the camel family, closely related to the llama. The meat is edible.

HUAYCHAO | A bird with a "flute-like" bill, said to be no bigger than a thrush, light gray, with white tail feathers that flutter when it sings. Probably a wren.

HUAYNO | A lively dance performed by groups of couples holding hands.

INCA | Name used to denote (1) the emperor, (2) the emperor's tribe, (3) the ruling class of the empire as a whole. (The plural is either "Inca" or "Incas.")

LLAMA | Member of the camel family, used principally as a beast of burden.

QUECHUA | The language of the Incas, still spoken by 5,000,000 people in Peru, Ecuador, Bolivia, and Argentina.

127

QUENUAL | A small tree (*Polylepis racemosa*), member of the rose family.

QUINOA | An herb (*Chenopodium quinoa*) grown for its seeds, used as a cereal.

TAHUANTINSUYU | "Land of the Four Quarters," the known world in its entirety.

VICUÑA | Member of the camel family, closely related to the llama, prized for its silky wool.

UTUSI | The chronicler Martín de Morúa writes: "Some say that utusi signifies the genital member, a word invented by lovers in the old days." Elsewhere he gives the translation "heart."

Quechua Pronunciation

Though the spelling of Quechua words has never been standardized, certain usages over the years have become more familiar than others. *Viracocha,* for example, is more often found than *Wiraqocha* or *Uirakocha.* In this book the familiar usages have been retained. At least some of the rules for pronunciation may be inferred by studying the following examples:

VIRACOCHA (weer-a-CO-cha)
VICUÑA (wee-COON-ya)
ATAHUALPA (a-ta-WAHL-pa)
CAHUILLACA (ca-weel-YA-ca)
LLOQUE YUPANQUI (lyo-kay yoo-PAHNG-kee)
HUAYNO (WY-no)
QUECHUA (KETCH-wa)
QUINOA (KEE-no-a)
QUENUAL (CANE-wahl)
YMA SUMAC (ee-ma SOO-mahk)
MAYTA CAPAC (my-ta CAH-pahk)
MAMA CAUA (ma-ma CAH-wa)

In a few cases the Spanish *j* has replaced the Quechua *s* and the Spanish, rather than the Quechua, pronunciation has become more usual: for example, Cajamarca (ca-ha-MAR-ka), Jauja (HOW-ha).

Note that all pronunciations given here are only approximate.

Suggestions for Further Reading

Arguedas, José María, and Stephan, Ruth. *The Singing Mountaineers.* 1957, University of Texas Press, Austin, Texas. An English-language anthology of contemporary Quechua lore: 41 lyrics, 9 stories, 2 essays by Arguedas, and an introduction by Stephan.

Brundage, Burr Cartwright. *Empire of the Inca.* 1963, University of Oklahoma Press, Norman, Okla. A reconstruction of Inca history, based on sixteenth- and seventeenth-century chronicles.

Mason, J. Alden. *The Ancient Civilizations of Peru.* 1957, revised edition 1968, Penguin Books, Inc., Baltimore, Md. An authoritative description of the Inca and pre-Inca cultures. Illustrated.

Osborne, Harold. *South American Mythology.* 1968, Paul Hamlyn, London. (Distributed in the United States by Leon Amiel, New York.) This book is largely devoted to the mythology of ancient Peru. Lavishly illustrated.

Prescott, William H. *History of the Conquest of Peru.* The classic account of Pizarro's conquest, first published in 1847. Many editions.